Flexible Working

Flexible Working

A STRATEGIC GUIDE TO SUCCESSFUL IMPLEMENTATION AND OPERATION

Stephen Simmons

KOGAN PAGE

First published in 1996

Kogan Page Limited
120 Pentonville Road
London N1 9JN

British Library Cataloguing in Publication Data
A CIP record for this book is available from the British Library.

ISBN 0 7494 1713 7

Typeset by Saxon Graphics Ltd, Derby
Printed and bound in Great Britain by Biddles Ltd, Guildford and Kings Lynn

Contents

Preface

This book deals with what flexible working is, why businesses need it, and how they implement it; it identifies all the main ingredients that go to make a successful flexible working implementation first as a trial, then as a general working tool.

The intention of the book is wholly practical; it is geared to the needs of those who wish to take the leap and do it, rather than to those undertaking theoretical research. In consequence, such topics as the potential benefits from flexible working, are discussed in terms of inducing decision makers to act, rather than of making a political case that flexible working is a good thing for the world. In the same vein technology issues are discussed at some length, because flexible working is heavily reliant on new technology if it is to work well, but the discussion is in management terms, not in technical terms.

Chapters 1 and 2 consist of an introduction describing what flexible working is; an assessment of the business case for why flexible working makes sense in business; and a discussion of the strategies for implementation that will show how best to go about introducing flexible working to your business.

Chapters 3 to 6 deal respectively with choosing tasks for flexible working; choosing people for flexible working; choosing locations for flexible working; and choosing equipment and services for flexible working. Chapters 7, 8 and 9 then deal with training issues; with implementing a flexible working trial; and with the longer-term future (post-trials) for flexible working in business.

Appendices include the trade union view; a full list of references used; a glossary of terms used; and a comprehensive bibliography of further reading.

For the benefit of the reader who has the task of creating a flexible working implementation and has little interest in theory or discussion, the book opens with an 'express implementation' guide for project managers, identifying key items (tick-marked in the text) for rapid project design.

Introduction

Flexible working methods have been gaining in popularity for some years now and have received very wide publicity: for many readers of this book, the intention will be to get under way with a flexible working scheme, rather than simply to find out more about it. For such readers, the flexible work project managers, an express implementation route is signposted through this book (by tick symbols in the right-hand margin). In conjunction with this note, the signposting identifies a quick route to assembling a management plan.

In Chapter 1, discussion of what flexible working is and of the background to it, relatively little is needed for an actual implementation; four main classifications of flexible work are identified in the section 'Forms of flexible work' (home based, centre based, mobile and drop-in centre) and these (or similar) groupings should at least gain a mention in the preamble to any proposed scheme. Even where a scheme is wholly based around one 'flavour' of flexible working (home-based telework, for instance) it is vital to keep in view the existence of other 'flavours' which are likely to become significant at some later stage.

By way of contrast with Chapter 1, the section on making the business case for flexible working (Chapter 2) contains a great deal that will be needed in writing a scheme proposal. The section 'The bottom line' establishes the need to identify and quantify 'benefits' (as opposed merely to describing the 'features' of flexible working from Chapter 1; features are interesting, but only benefits make a case for implementation). A series of examples (2.1; 2.2; 2.3; 2.4; and 2.5) quantifying specific benefits may help to jog the memory as to where the financial gains might lie, and some back-up data (Figures 2.1 and 2.2) provide the raw figures from which to build a specific argument. The 'Audit of impacts' will help to assemble this into a rational order for calculation, and a very simplified minimum presentation is shown in the 'Sample executive summary', 'Sample description of the pilot scheme', 'Sample budget' and 'Sample implementation timetable' formats. Many businesses will have standardised in-house formats for such presentations, of course, and a very high standard of presentation using tools like Power Point from Microsoft or Freelance Graphics from Lotus clearly would be appropriate for a scheme which is likely to feature quite advanced personal computer (PC) and technology uses.

In the context of project management and scheme design, the next few chapters are effectively appendices to Chapter 2. In Chapter 3, the question of the appropriateness of flexible working to businesses of various different sizes; in various different industry sectors; and in handling tasks of various different natures, are all discussed, in order to help home in on the best and most fruitful area in which to initiate a project. 'Choosing the general field' raises the important question of pre-existing 'tacit' flexible working. Of the numerous tables classifying existing flexible work implementations, Figure 3.4 is a key reminder of where, to date, the most fruitful areas have been, and the section 'Job analysis in detail' extends this into a checklist format for project managers.'The 'Job analysis audit' and its accompanying 'Other criteria' for decision making complete sufficient material for the justification of choice of tasks; and for the justification that flexible work is an appropriate technique for the specific business being discussed.

Chapter 4 is concerned with the vital question of choice of staff for flexible working. A number of differing but complementary views of the specific traits of personality to be looked for in flexible working personnel are combined into a single grouping in the section 'Personal characteristics — the company view', as characteristics of time management; motivation management; communication management; lifestyle management and technology management. The questions arising in handling staff before and during an implementation are discussed in the sections 'Warming up' and 'Asking questions of staff', where checklists are provided of what information to convey to staff and what information to seek from staff. Where an implementation will involve self-employed or outsourced functions, as well as, or instead of, directly employed staff, then the section 'Codes of conduct and practice' will help to identify some of the means of control that will be indicated.

Questions related to the location of work follow on directly from those related to the employment of staff and/or contractors. Within Chapter 5, many minor issues and side-shows that follow from dispersed activity (planning consents etc) are identified in the 'Introduction' to the chapter. Much of the chapter naturally looks at questions relating to home working, since the home is statistically the most common location in flexible working. A listing of types of premises other than 'the office' or 'the home' is given in 'Agile workplaces', and (as described in the introduction to this chapter) it is important to bear these alternatives in mind in any scheme, even if they are not currently to be implemented.

For home-based flexible working the section 'Home offices' defines very fully the criteria for acceptance of a particular home environment as suitable for flexible working. It does this in terms of performance rather than of features, so that a rational assessment of locations can be achieved in the 'Locational audit': this is a particularly important point, in that it will assuredly be necessary at some stage to reject a particular location, and this will need to be handled in a non-personalised way if giving offence is to be avoided. Since the change of contract terms with personnel will be more concerned with location than with anything else, a 'Checklist for terms' and a suggested draft letter amending contract terms 'The no change, no worsening agreement' are quoted at this stage.

Flexible working has been enabled largely by new technology developments, and designing a flexible work project is still very much concerned with the appropriate choice of technologies. These are surveyed in Chapter 6, which opens with a checklist of the very large range available for flexible working purposes. For a project manager, much of this will be well-trodden ground, so it is primarily the newer topics of bandwidth, and its drivers such as video-conferencing and screen-sharing that will be of interest, and those are grouped together in the section 'Bandwidth and innovative services', immediately before the other current driver for increasing bandwidth, 'The Internet'. Two areas where old and well-established techniques have extended only recently into applications particularly suited to flexible working are integrated services digital network (ISDN), in the context of small switches (the section 'Wide area networks and LAN interconnect') and mobile networks, in the context of group services mobile (GSM) use for data transmission (the 'Mobile networks — satellite, radio and cellular telephony'). Finally, it may be appropriate to look at newer developments in the good old-fashioned public switched telephone network (PSTN) system, particularly in 'Virtual private networks' (VPNs).

It is extraordinarily unlikely that any new flexible working implementations will succeed without proper attention to training. Chapter 7, 'Training and encouraging — what competences are needed?' summarises the likely options for training needs for different groups of individuals, and subsequently categorises them as task based; operational; personal; or group competences. Checklists for specific training topics within these categories are provided in each case, so that customisation of training requirements for individual implementations can be undertaken. There is a complex inter-linkage between the training areas of flexible working and the formalisation of quality management and the section on 'Quality management issues' shows one way in which the existence of a set of quality procedures can be utilised to identify areas in which further training may be required, and also to provide a format for such training.

At first glance, having completed a review of Chapters 1 to 7, that might appear to be all that is needed. However, 'getting it right' is rarely enough: it is also necessary to be seen to get it right, to be seen by the right people to get it right and, even after the event, to report in such a way as to be seen to have got it right.

Chapter 8 concerns itself with the strategies needed to make an implementation work most effectively: 'Strategic review' checklists all the people who have to be 'sold' on the subject within a business, and 'Championing and beyond' discusses championing as a means to achieving this 'hearts and minds' function. Because the initial stages of implementation tend to be concerned with overcoming perceived obstacles (in many businesses there exist people whose sole function seems to be the perceiving of obstacles), Figures 8.1 and 8.2, which identify respectively the employer's and employee's view of what constitutes an obstacle, are most important in designing a project which will inevitably be as much concerned with selling flexible working as with doing it. Project managers can convince themselves easily that they should be concerned only with doing, not with selling, but the section 'Activities within a trial' should help greatly to overcome that view. Finally, 'A checklist for teleworking trials' checklists the activities within a project from an organisational standpoint.

The chapter concerned with future developments naturally offers less of interest to those planning action today but even so it would be appropriate to have in mind the shape of 'Tomorrow's businesses' in respect of being loosely located, loosely defined, widely informed, proactively run and trading in new 'stuff'.

Finally, Appendix A (The Trade Union View) is obligatory reading for all those contemplating any sort of flexible working project involving existing staff in an existing business, and is recommended even where outsourced staff are involved.

The intention is that any manager following the 'tick' route through this should be equipped with the bare bones of the information needed for successful implementation of flexible working.

Chapter 1

Flexible working and teleworking

Flexible working and teleworking

lexible working is independent of office formalities, office hours and office locations: teleworking is essentially communications-based flexible working. These are quite soft-edged, nebulous concepts, not easily tied down with definitions. A good way to think of flexible working is as part of a continuum of ways of working that includes shop working, factory working, office working and now flexible working. Some common questions about (teleworking and) flexible working might be understood by substituting, say, office working into them, thus:

For	What exactly do flexible workers do?
Read	What exactly do office workers do?
For	How do I become a flexible worker?
Read	How do I become an office worker?
For	Surely flexible working isn't really important?
Read	Surely office working isn't really important?

According to current European Community (EC) research, 4.8 per cent of the UK workforce was involved in flexible working for at least one day per week in 1994, and the rate of increase is about 25–30 per cent per annum. Most flexible workers are only actually teleworking for some part of the time: on average about 50 per cent of their time is spent working at home, 25 per cent working in their clients' offices and 25 per cent on the move (trains, hotels etc). These are average figures, not figures for any one individual, but they do make the point that there are a variety of ways of going about this flexible working business. It is possible to produce wildly varying statistics about flexible working simply by making differing assumptions: one recent UK academic study claimed that the whole subject of flexible working was of no socioeconomic consequence because only 53,000 individuals were involved — but the study had defined flexible working as being about full-time workers only, at home for 100 per cent of working time only, who were exclusively permanent employees of one company only, and who were totally reliant on telecommmunications in order to be able to work. This naturally excluded those who worked at home sometimes, in hotels sometimes, on the move, under contract or really just about everybody who is flexible working in real life situations. What is to be learned from their study is not that flexible working does not matter, it is that the old idea of the straightforward 'job' is being radically challenged by the spread of flexible working; work is a less rigidly structured activity than it ever used to be. It is a mistake to think of flexible working as just another name for teleworking — there is much more to it than that, although teleworking is often a major component of it.

Telecommuting and outsourcing

One striking aspect of flexible working as at 1995 is the uneven distribution of its take-up when related to the size of business. In broad terms, one half of all flexible workers are in businesses with more than 100 employees, and the other half are in businesses with less than 50 employees: there is a null zone of business size (50–100) where flexible working is virtually non-existent. There is no need for our purposes to attempt any very precise definition of the boundaries of this null zone, but accurate figures are quoted in the *Final Report of the TELDET Project*.[1] There is wide acceptance that the null zone derives from the existence of two very distinct entry routes into flexible working. The first route is a 'top down' large corporate implementation mode (*telecommuters*) in which a board level decision is taken to 'flexible work' (as a transitive verb) a group of employees. This (generally) is associated with large businesses. The second route, which is generally associated with individuals and particularly with micro small and medium sized enterprises (SMEs), is a lifestyle change mode (*telemercenaries* and *teleguerrillas* in the USA) in which an individual professional or employee (or sometimes a small cohesive business or department) opts for flexible working not only as a change of lifestyle but also coincidentally as a change from direct employment to some form of contracting. Over the last ten years or so the corporate, top-down implementations of flexible working have trickled down from the pioneers among very large corporates (Xerox, ICL etc) into more modest-sized companies, while many of the early flexible working micro-SMEs have grown larger and become medium-sized businesses. However, there still remains a null zone between the two patterns, albeit a zone that is shrinking in size. For the corporate manager, this translates into a choice between *in-house* flexible working implementation, where the work is handled primarily by existing staff and only the methods change, or an *out-sourcing* implementation, where the work is done by an independent contractor or contractors (albeit that the contractors actually may have worked as direct employees of the business previously).

Years of heavy publicity for the concept of teleworking and subsequently for the generality of flexible working have led to a common misconception (particularly among unemployed people) that it is possible to 'go into flexible working' as if it were a career option. In fact, as the foregoing indicates, most flexible workers will have had some prior 'non-flexible' working relationship with those who are now their employers or their clients. Their career choice was to 'go into insurance' or to 'go into publishing' and not at all to 'go into flexible working' which is really just a particular mode of delivery for their work.

Forms of flexible work

Whatever the history and job status of the individual carrying out the work, there are four main modes of flexible working, defined according to organisational, technical, timing and legal criteria:

- **Home-based (telework).** This consists of working from home rather than from the normal or previous place of work, using communication and information technologies to accomplish tasks and to remain in contact with the one (or possibly several) business or businesses in the flexible worker's portfolio of clients or employers. Home-telework is often carried out in alternation (one to three days per week) with an activity carried out at the site of the client business itself; this is sometimes referred to as 'alternating telework' and is probably the most common of all flexible work modes. ✓
- **Satellite office/touchdown/drop-in centre.** This mode of flexible work refers to the operation of a relatively autonomous unit ✓

within one company which, although possibly separated geographically from the parent company, is in contact with it through a telecommunications link; in practice it can be almost indistinguishable from a conventional branch office. Given sufficiently good communications, it can be also almost indistinguishable from being physically located within a 'Head Office', but characteristically there will be no, or few, individually designated offices within it.

- **Nomad telework, mobile or itinerant work.** This applies mainly to individual professionals and, most frequently, sales/technical representatives whose work requires intensive travel and who, by means of electronic communication, can both remain in contact with their base and link up with the client companies using their services wherever they may be; it is the second most prevalent telework mode. ✓

- **Neighbourhood office/telecentre.** These facilities bring together a weight of electronic information and telecommunications equipment (eg PC, fax etc) shared by users who may be employed by different companies, or by small firms and independent teleworkers for whom such an investment would be undesirable on their own. The centres are often located in close proximity to the teleworker's place of residence and also may be used for other activities such as telesecretarial services, telephone and telematic services, teletraining, teletranslation etc. Some telecentres themselves employ teleworkers. They differ from satellite offices in not being owned by, or tied to, one business. Telecottage is an alternative name which, by historical accident, tends to be associated with such ventures when initially funded by, for example, development agencies or local authorities; however, the 'green' implications of the word can lead to its acquiring a social rather than commercial implication which may not necessarily be well received at board level in potential client businesses. The Virtual Office is one major commercial operation of this type (in Piccadilly, London) whose name is copyright and so not available for new implementations. ✓

Flexible work not flexible jobs

Just as the flexible work mode is independent of the history and job status of the individual flexible worker, so also is flexible working concerned with the achievement of value adding tasks rather than the mere 'possession' of a job, again independently of history or job status. The idea of the 'job' (and, more particularly, that of unemployment) is so dominant in our thinking today that it is hard to remember that 'jobs' have actually only been the norm for a few hundred years, and even then, in only a few parts of the world. In tribal societies, for instance, individuals may do work, but they probably do not have jobs: servitude is more commonly achieved by force, not by payment. The concept of employment, as opposed to slavery or domestic servitude, was given its impetus mainly by the Industrial Revolution. At first the difference between slavery and employment was marginal, so that in the eighteenth century, 'factory', 'school', 'workhouse' and 'prison' were often largely indistinguishable physically, but by the mid-nineteenth century, there were 15 million paid employees in the UK (of whom 2 million were in fact unemployed). Machines necessitated workers: the growing size and complexity of machines necessitated the factory and the mill, to which workers had to go. In turn, towns and cities grew around the factories and the population moved from countryside to town to service the factories. All this happened very quickly over the course of perhaps only about 250 years: it is important to remember that this socioeconomic phenomenon is quite recent and is not necessarily irreversible. In this light, flexible working is an important issue for politicians but the same concepts are also by no means irrelevant to human resource managers; flexible working often reverses the old historic movement of people, so that the flow is from town to countryside — albeit a much modified countryside capable of sustaining modern communications. Flexible working can free businesses from the constraints of working in towns and cities, to their benefit and that of their staff.

From an organisational viewpoint, flexible working clearly lends itself to service-based activities, rather than to production-based activities, so that it may, at first glance, seem to do little in the way of replacing the concept of the industrial city. However, productivity in the creation of goods has increased vastly in recent years, at least in good part through the recognition that services supporting production (design, sales etc) can be separated out and handled in fundamentally different ways from production itself. The activities that can be supported by flexible working are in fact a very high proportion of all such working tasks, including those:

- Consisting primarily of the collection, processing and creation of information, where this is performed using information technology.

- Involving those specific applications and communications requirements or tasks, which can be fully supported by telecommunications.
- Which can be organised either separately for individual flexible workers (which would normally imply high added value), or are common to a number of flexible workers at lower added values, whether these are of a permanent or temporary nature.
- Involving geographical locations at significant distances from the employer: including locations which are in fact mobile 'platforms'. (A mobile platform might be a van equipped as a workshop, or it might equally as likely be a car or train with a mobile phone or notebook PC).

Within such broad generic task areas there are some specific activities which are particularly commonplace. The *European Telecommunications Handbook for Teleworkers*[2] (published by the EC) identifies some specific activities under the headings of:

- Telesecretary.
- Teletranslation.
- Teleconsulting.
- Teledesign.
- Teledocumentation.
- Telediagnosis.

These examples are discussed in more detail below, taking the EC definitions of these activities as a base. It is worth noting that, for example, although an activity such as teletranslation is well established and commonplace, the use of the word 'teletranslation' itself is not commonplace. The various 'tele-' terms are useful concepts, but have no real-world applicability as common terminology.

Example 1.1

Telesecretary

The functions of a telesecretary cover standard secretarial tasks such as data capture, text processing and also frequently telephone reception, together with more sophisticated tasks such as desk top publishing (DTP). Good networking facilities can allow telesecretary bases to support other flexible working activities (for example, teletranslation or telemanagement) to create a full range of administration services, meeting the needs both of, large companies aiming to externalise and subcontract secretarial services, and also of SMEs and professionals who normally cannot afford the complete integration of such services within their own organisational structure.

Telesecretarial service offices may be located in rural areas or suburban areas where human resources are more available and less expensive (particularly in the presence of grant aid) without losing direct contact with their customers.

Functional analysis of telesecretary activity

- A client telephones to the telesecretary's voice mailbox to dictate letters and to request telephone calls (change of meetings, reservations) to be made by the secretarial service.
- The telesecretarial staff make telephone calls as required and leave the result within the client's voice mailbox.
- They also type the letters and forward them to the recipients (by mail), or return them to the client via file transfer applications if corrections and/or signature are required.

Tools and techniques

Clearly, in order to allow working closely with the client (for example, making corrections to documents) compatible computer and telecommunications tools are essential. A common set of communications tools, and training to use them, has to be built into any telesecretarial scheme. For this reason, telesecretary–client relationships are likely to be long-term orientated (to cover the setting-up costs). The main communication activities therefore normally will be limited to a relatively unchanging set of partners. Even though the telesecretary service does not depend on physical proximity, most teleservice centres work on a regional level (because face-to-face contacts are difficult to replace totally). National or transborder applications do, however, occur in special services (eg translation).

Telesecretary activities can be managed in many ways, from the single individual to the networking of satellite centres. Employees of telesecretarial services can work from home or from telecentres, and this type of work is particularly well suited to special needs employment.

Adapted (with the permission of the EC) from the *European Telecommunications Handbook for Teleworkers.*[2]

Example 1.2

Teletranslation

With the increasing internationalisation of trading, the demand for document translation (contracts, specifications etc) and for rare linguistic competences (Mandarin, etc) increases steadily. This demand is increasingly fulfilled by SMEs offering teletranslation services. In this context, it is necessary to distinguish between interpreting (vocal) and translation (text) services, although both types of service give companies access to specialised translators and/or interpreters regardless of their geographical location.

Functional analysis of teletranslation activity

- The client sends the document (to be translated) by fax, file transfer or simply by mail, depending on urgency.
- The document is forwarded by the teleservice centre to a qualified translator, quite possibly in another country.
- The document is returned to the customer as a text file, a DTP document on file, or as a paper copy etc.

As a specific example, an answer to an international invitation to a tender is produced using a word processing programme by a company's own in-house staff; then sent by fax to the teleservice company which forwards it to the translator. The translator returns the translated document directly to the customer via E-mail file transfer which enables the client to carry out any further processing and printing. Necessary corrections can be made interactively with the help of joint working tools (these joint viewing or editing procedures necessitate ISDN connections on both sides; the technique is commonly handled by whiteboarding software), by E-mail, or by voice conversation by phone.

Tools and techniques

Teletranslators have to possess a wide range of transfer modes and network accesses to cover the likely range of specific customer needs and facilities.

Adapted (with the permission of the EC) from the *European Telecommunications Handbook for Teleworkers*.[2]

Example 1.3

Teleconsulting

This type of teleservice supports its client businesses with general administrative guidance and special services (eg accounting) at a distance. For example, a French management services organisation offering consultancy to farmers (3300 members) has organised its services into a wholly decentralised structure with regional satellite offices, offering such services as joint procurement of foodstuffs, seed etc.

Functional analysis of teleconsulting activity

- Farmers, equipped with terminals connected to the regional office via PSTN, send information (eg an order or, turnover figures) to the teleconsultants' mailbox.
- The regional office collates the orders from farmers and creates aggregated orders (to obtain better purchase conditions for the farmers), with acknowledgements via PSTN.
- The regional office forwards the accounting figures via ISDN to the central office where the data is processed (for example for tax, subsidy and income calculations).
- The accountancy results (administrative papers including comments and suggestions) are returned to the regional office via ISDN file transfer, and the regional offices distribute the printed documents to the farmers and tax authorities respectively, via PSTN.

Tools and techniques

In order to speed the information exchange between central and satellite offices, the transfer of processed accounting data is a totally automated procedure. The regional office periodically initiates file requests from the central office in order to recover prepared records of (client) farmers' data. In this case, ISDN is used to cope with the high volume of data and the frequency of file and document transfer, while the transfer of farmers' data from the regional to the central office is carried out via PSTN.

Adapted (with the permission of the EC) from the *European Telecommunications Handbook for Teleworker.*[2]

Example 1.4

Teledesign

Teledesign applications were developed primarily as an outsourcing activity to overcome the high costs of in-house work and to relieve skills shortages. Advanced image processing tools such as computer aided design (CAD) (for technical drawings) and DTP (for logos, symbols, titling etc) depend on expert skills and high-level information technology which necessitate high investment costs. Specialised service companies or freelance professionals respond to this demand by offering high performance editing of documents, brochures and drawings. Several distributed clients can thereby effectively share scarce resources and expensive equipment at a distance. Teledesign can shorten the production process and offers the potential for both productivity and flexibility to increase.

Functional analysis of teledesign activity

- The client sends the design concept sketches via mail or fax to the teledesign centre.
- The teledesign centre, which has at its disposal a set of high performance computers, digitises the sketches for subsequent manipulation by CAD tools.
- The subcontractors responsible for production of different subsets of the project design are sent the appropriate data via ISDN or PSTN and return their work in the same way. The teledesign services then works with the company's lead designer to make amendments and finalise the work.

Tools and techniques

This service represents considerable hard- and software investments, and continual updating of skills and tools. Its use is necessarily restricted to a limited number of customers and tends therefore to be associated with very close subcontracting relationships between the teledesign service and its clients, and often also in turn between the service and its subcontractors.

Adapted (with the permission of the EC) from the *European Telecommunications Handbook for Teleworker*.[2]

Example 1.5

Document handling services (teledocumentation)

Large corporates (and government agencies) operating at national or international level are often faced with the problem of establishing and organising the efficient flow of large volumes of information between different departments and services. This is true of departments widely dispersed over one or several countries, but applies equally to salespeople and agents travelling widely on behalf of their companies. Teledocumentation services help to move information about a company's products and services, can forward client requirements from the company's product line management to its regional sales offices or mobile workers, and can handle clients' orders taken by its field personnel.

For obvious reasons, national telephone companies have been among the first to implement teledocumentation services: in the specific example discussed, the teledocumentation service (as a sales support) acts as the marketing interface between the product line management (at head office level) and the regional sales engineers who may be travelling around (ie at local level).

Functional analysis of teledocumentation activity

The tasks performed consist of analysing, elaborating and validating solutions to customers' complex communication problems. Within this, the experts have to handle a considerable amount of information (commercial instructions, tariffs, construction details, market analysis etc) which must be reliable and therefore continuously updated. The service provides a remotely accessible database for this purpose, which allows:

- the establishment of local databases (satellite offices), exactly replicating the available data on the central database, regularly updated via ISDN (this is the first step to the installation of a distributed database document management system);
- the remote retrieval and collection of information, eg the mobile salesperson or agent who negotiates at the client's site can connect his or her portable via PSTN, either to the satellite office or to the central host, to collect information needed for his or her consultancy tasks;
- direct (on-line) remote access via ISDN to specific documents and their transmission via file transfer.

Tools and techniques

The central base undertakes the creation, management and updating of the database. The document retrieval procedure consists of server calling, transmission demand, research, document transfer and storage. Document and file exchange require medium data transmission rates and the use of data compression software. At the central base the computer and telecommunication facilities represent high fixed costs (server, scanner, database management system, CD-ROM, data compression), whereas the investment required in satellite office equipment is relatively low (desktop and portable computers to interface database applications, ISDN-connection for the satellite office to main office link, modems for the mobile workers).

In general, central and distributed document management systems are being implemented at both national and international levels. The management of such databases, because of their high fixed costs, is now frequently outsourced to independent teleservice provision.

Adapted (with the permission of the EC) from the *European Telecommunications Handbook for Teleworkers.*[2]

Example 1.6

Telediagnostics (or telemedicine)

Telediagnostics enables real time collaboration between professionals (and particularly medical professionals) at widely dispersed locations in order to solve specific problems. The key issue here is the availability of, and access to, scarce expert knowledge and skills, crossing institutional and geographic boundaries, so as to facilitate, for example, home-care treatment in remote areas. Expert collaboration is enhanced by the sharing of medical images, records, data, voice and video (in real time) in order to discuss difficult cases between several specialists. The medical expert consulted can utilise the information available at the host (usually a hospital) with colleagues in the hospital and on-the-spot with the patient.

Functional analysis of telemedicine activities

- Consultation of specialised medical databases in order to improve and speed up diagnosis (eg browsing of medical images, records or video explaining the characteristics of a disease).
- Medical data transfer (eg remote data processing, test analysis by specialised research centres, specialist advice on interpreting X-rays etc).
- Distributing and dispatching patient dossiers between several departments (surgery, pathology laboratories, etc).
- Integration of different remote medical units/experts in order to improve diagnostic procedure (central hospital, to regional health centre, to specialised or national research centres, to international centres of excellence).

Tools and techniques

Telediagnostics requires transmission facilities for a variety of media types (text, image, voice, video and graphics). Video and multimedia are essential in what is necessarily a broadband communications area.

Communication between experts on a shared information basis can be aided by groupware tools, for instance, in the creation and exchange of multimedia messages in order to enable the remote consultation and review of patient records. These messages may then be transferred to a specific remote recipient. The distribution of multimedia patient medical records require broadband networks and good data compression. For access to, and the forwarding of, medical data, high speed local area networks (LANs) are required (within and between hospitals). Consultation of an external expert or of a remote database will normally require an ISDN link.

Adapted (with the permission of the EC) from the *European Telecommunications Handbook for Teleworkers*.[2]

Example 1.7

Programming

Software development is one of the best-known examples of flexible work applications. From the early 1980s onwards, large corporates began to implement flexible work projects for programmers and for software and systems specialists, both within Europe and utilising Indian and Asian resources. There are several reasons for the importance of flexible work in such applications:

- Programming and system development tasks are particularly susceptible to being broken down into manageable, individual steps, ie they are structured and planned. The use of formal planning methods is intrinsic in tasks of this nature. Thus the organisational prerequisites for flexible work are to a large degree already met, and individual work procedure steps can easily be separated out from the overall development process and carried out remotely. Collaboration and job sharing with colleagues is co-ordinated by means of formal planning and project management tools.
- These tasks require a high degree of personal concentration, which typically is easier to achieve in the relaxed atmosphere of the home or of a satellite office than, for example, in a city centre office, to which daily commuting also may be a serious problem.
- The workers, software and systems specialists, are highly-qualified specialists who place a premium on creative freedom and free time allocation (both characteristics of flexible work), and skills shortages have given them the negotiating power to achieve those lifestyle aspirations.

There are a wide variety of tasking areas in teleprogramming; including software development for applications or system software; systems analysis and maintenance tasks; and there are associated non-programming tasks such as technical authorship (of manuals etc) which have developed in parallel. Groups of programmers, rather than individuals, normally will be involved in the development process, necessitating special provisions to deal with joint usage of resources (eg libraries) and to ensure the consistency and interoperability of individual program modules.

The teleprogrammer's teleworkplace needs more than just to be equipped with those software development tools required for the task in hand. Good communications with colleagues and supervisors in the central office are vital for ensuring continuous consultation on work progress and work results, and for the discussion of technical questions as they arise. This normally includes the use of E-mail and office communications systems, as well as joint access to project management tools.

In organisational terms, teleprogramming is generally conducted at home or in satellite/neighbourhood offices. As an example of teleprogramming in satellite offices a Swiss bank has set up eight satellite offices that, to date, have taken over 10 per cent of its entire software development department.

In teleprogramming, there are numerous examples of international activity involving the transfer of programming tasks outside national borders, either within Europe or overseas. The time-zone difference between Europe and the USA is exploited in order to achieve 'around-the-clock' utilisation of central data processing resources (with host systems in the USA and Europe). As the developers in, say, Ireland wind down their working day, their colleagues in the USA are just beginning theirs.

Adapted (with the permission of the EC) from the *European Telecommunications Handbook for Teleworkers*.[2]

Hot desking

It is surely no surprise to anyone that many of the companies which were first to pick up the concepts of flexible working and run with them, were within the computer industry. The Digital Equipment corporation, within the life span of one man, has gone from tiny start-up through massive growth to industry dinosaur; and then through near-failure to total re-engineering and rebirth as a flexible work corporation, light-footed and responsive enough to survive against its younger competitors in the (very much red in tooth and claw) computer jungle.

In the course of this it went through a phase of having large and opulent offices in most countries in the developed world, but now its ideas of what is appropriate in the way of office provision are radically different. On page 34 is the company's description of its 'Flexible Finland' concept in Helsinki, probably the first major implementation of hot desking. Given that it included an office sauna, this really is hot desking. Chapter 5 (locations) looks at other hot desking, touch-down centre and drop-in centre modes of flexible working of which this is just one example.

Example 1.8

Hot desking in Digital Finland

In January 1988 60 people from Digital Finland Sales and Service moved into the 'office of the future', the features of which were:

- no ownership of desk space but easy access to any facility that individuals might need, whether a quiet room, terminal, telephone or meeting room;
- garden swings (the best four-person conference room there is and a way of bringing the home atmosphere into the office);
- video and hi-fi sets; murals along one wall;
- kitchen facilities, tables and chairs to relax at and enjoy a snack;
- a water fountain; a sauna, to which customers are invited.

Benefits

- Space savings of 40 per cent, compared to the traditional Finnish office, despite allocating 25 per cent of office space to areas of relaxation and recreation. Costs associated with refurbishment, supplying new equipment, some furnishings and mobile storage-trolleys were offset by the savings in space and the improvements in productivity and business.
- Salesperson productivity increased by up to 30 per cent.
- Significant increase in recorded sales.
- Reduced employee attrition. There was no attrition from the 'office of the future' during the financial year after it was established.
- Improved communication. Partitions were removed and there were no dedicated work places. Because individuals move around from space to space, they meet a greater number of people and understand their jobs. Decision making is better and access to individuals is easier.
- There was job enrichment for secretaries and administration staff as they became the hub of the office. Secretaries work more as a team. They can add value to customers because they can answer questions on behalf of all senior managers and they have more flexibility themselves. In fact, secretaries have large desks and senior managers have much smaller desks projecting off these.

Chapter 2

The business case for flexible working

The bottom line

What is in it for me? Having acquired some idea of what flexible working is, there will be little point in proceeding further if there seems to be no prospect of some benefit accruing. Obviously, given the wide variety of forms that flexible working can take, then there is an equally wide variety of benefits that can potentially flow from it. It is tempting to split the benefits into, first, direct 'financial benefits', and then 'other benefits' (quality of life, for instance) but in doing so it is important not to lose sight of the fact that most benefits are ultimately likely to impact on the bottom line. Benefits (including 'quality of life' benefits) which act to increase motivation and performance levels, or to decrease staff turnover rates, ultimately can produce very substantial financial gain. In this respect it is interesting that many corporates which have implemented flexible working principally in order to reduce costs, have then found that the main benefit has arisen through gains in productivity rather than through reduced costs: in making the business case prior to first implementation, however, the easily quantified cost savings are often more convincing than the less easily predictable productivity gains. The first activity, then, is to assess the likely benefits arising, before moving on to try to optimise the presentation of the business case for change. Preparing any individual business case is likely to involve concentrating on a single specific financial benefit, but it is important to realise that the long-term business case is about competitiveness, and even quite possibly survival. Without flexible working, failure may well follow in the middle (five year) term.

Benefits and drawbacks

Assessing which perceived benefits and drawbacks are real and quantifiable can be problematic, as noted above, but the perceptions of those who have already implemented, or are considering implementing, flexible working do at least give forewarning of how the presentation of the business case might be received. Among the benefits and drawbacks most frequently cited are those on this listing (adapted from one by Paul Vallery and Christian Wolmar, quoted in *The Independent* newspaper of 18 July 1995):

Benefits	**Drawbacks**
Reduced costs	Increased training needs
Greater convenience	Potential technical problems
Greater flexibility	Cost of equipment
Better retention of skilled staff	Potential communication difficulties
Easier recruitment of skilled staff	Key staff unavailability for *ad hoc* meetings
Greater productivity/efficiency	Difficulty of management
Better customer service	Risk of poor quality work
Less travel problems	Risk of social isolation and losing touch
Better for the environment	Fear of creating a bad impression
Employment of disabled staff	Fear of lack of career development
Employment of staff with childcare responsibilities	Risk of lack of loyalty to the business
Employment of other carers	Potential insurance problems
Less stress on the workforce	
Space saving/avoidance of relocation	

Productivity and efficiency

In many departments of businesses, and in some whole industries, productivity is measured by the equation:

Efficiency = Production quantity divided by labour time.

This simplistic view neglects any consideration of space usage, overheads and so on, but is nonetheless commonplace (the number of man-hours needed to build a car seems to have become a totemic figure in the motor industry, for example). However, once this time efficiency rises to anything like its maximum, the distinctions involved in changing it become too fine to be usable, and efficiency and productivity gains become dependent on:

- less space usage;

- less travel;
- less management;
- less general overhead.

In these cases the equation becomes:

Efficiency = total production divided by total activity

and then, very often, lower working times will not impact on productivity significantly.

The significance of this for the flexible working business case is that the latter, more complex, equation for measuring productivity has to be the measure used if the productivity gains of flexible working are to become apparent.

Direct financial benefits

Cost savings on office space usage

In most cost analyses of flexible working, office space has had the largest single cost impact; there is obviously always a flexible work reduction in the costs of office space — with employees from companies moving to alternative office space (such as the home) less office space will be needed at the main office, with the resulting benefit of rental cost savings (assuming that companies do not simply end up with empty office space for which they have to pay anyway, eg because of inflexible lease arrangements). A typical summary cost saving on this rental element is presented in Example 2.1, adapted from an actual case study.

Example 2.1

Example: ten staff previously occupying 150 sq ft each, now working at home for four days a week and desk-sharing at the office one day a week; 1500 sq ft of head office space becomes available to be reused but, offsetting this, an extra cost per person of £300 per annum arises for home 'rent'.

1500 sq ft × £40 = £60,000 pa × 90% saving	= £54,000
10 home allowances × £300 = £ 3000 pa new cost	= £3000
Saving (10 staff)	**£51,000**

Cost savings on car park usage

There may also be a reduction in the cost of expensive city parking space — land previously set aside for employee parking can then be put to better use. This often neglected on-cost can in fact be very substantial: one car effectively occupies about 375 sq ft of premium space, albeit not always within a building. At the least, however, this is likely to cost £1500 per annum in a central location, and a more typical figure would be £2500.

Other office facilities savings

Cost savings from reduced office use are not necessarily confined to the rental/capital costs area, but may have other substantial elements. The figures in Figure 2.1 are derived from the *Times-Procord Office Costs Index*[1] for 1995, and indicate the scale of the potential savings to be made in this area.

Example 2.2

Example: based on ten staff as in Example 2.1.

3750 sq ft × £4 = £15,000 × 80% saving	£12,000
Costs for car parking at home	nil
Saving (10 staff)	**£12,000**

Note: This is very nearly 25 per cent of the office rental savings in Example 2.1.

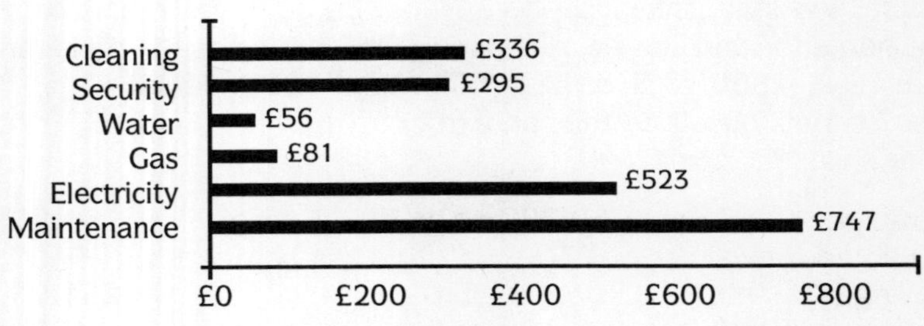

Figure 2.1 *Office overheads: annual costs per employee*

While there is no reason to assume that electricity, gas and water usage will be any less (so that in practice an allowance equal to the £660 annual cost shown above is likely to be paid), maintenance, security, and cleaning are, in total, likely to cost substantially less than their £1375 average total cost within office facilities.

Example 2.3

Example: based on ten staff as in Example 2.1.

10 × £1375 saved on maintenance etc	£13,750
10 × £200 allowances given	£ 2000
Saving (10 staff)	**£11,750**

Note: Again, this is close to 25 per cent of the office rental saving in Example 2.1.

While it is much more difficult to quantify savings in other office support items (messengers and such like), the significant costs that arise in offices under these headings should also come into the equation when considering the business costs for flexible working. The costs shown in Figure 2.2 (also derived from the *Times-Procord Office Costs Index*[1]) are potentially relevant.

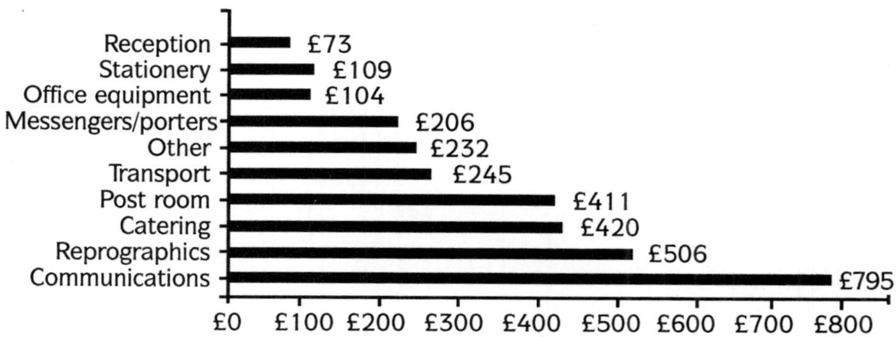

Figure 2.2 *Costs of office support items*

Increased amount of working capital

In addition to the more obvious savings, there can be a very substantial improvement in working capital requirements arising from rejigging the use of real estate: annual savings on rental or ownership may well be accompanied by further savings from reduced costs of borrowing. This can aggregate the initial rental savings considerably.

Example 2.4

Example 2.1	rental savings (net)	£51,000
Example 2.2	car parking extra cost	£12,000
Example 2.3	maintenance etc costs	£11,750
Example 2.4	5% of the above for financing	£3750
Saving (10 staff)		**£78,500**

This would be an appropriate figure for an inner-city organisation with prestige offices, and is taken before considering any extra costs arising from extra equipment or support/training requirements. A survey by Warwick University for the Economic and Social Research Council (July 1995) suggested that net savings figures between £1500 and £3000 per employee per annum are typically achieved in practice, after allowing for the total additional costs necessarily arising in implementation.

Indirect financial benefits

Better retention of staff

With the associated increase in living standards and motivation there comes a substantial decrease in staff turnover. In fact this also includes a direct benefit in reduced recruiting costs: however, those quantitative survey results related to staff turnover reductions that have been published to date have almost invariably been related simply to the life-time of a specific project, so that projecting forward hard figures for overall savings is difficult. In consequence the emphasis in making the business case generally falls on the indirect benefit of increased productivity and reduced in-house training costs arising from lower staff turnover. This is particularly crucial in businesses where staff have high skills levels, and doubly so where those skills are rare or in high demand. Recruitment costs are more readily quantified from in-house or published data. A typical example is shown in Example 2.5.

Example 2.5

Ten staff as in Example 2.1.

Previous turnover per annum	17.5% of workforce per annum
Costs 10 × 0.175 × £3800 for recruitment	£6650
Turnover for flexible working staff	10% of workforce per annum
Costs 10 × 0.1 × £3800 for recruitment	£3800
Saving (10 staff)	**£2850**

Reduced sick leave

A striking example of the incidental benefits that arise from flexible working is the following (Example 2.6), quoted in the book *Teleworking Explained*[2].

One of the reasons cited for reductions in sick leave is that commuting may be a very much more difficult undertaking for the unwell or convalescent than is their actual work, so that working at home, even for the whole working day, may be attainable where commuting is not. Additionally, there is a substantial benefit from working at a reduced level at home (eg with flu) for the flexible worker as opposed to not working at all for the absentee office worker. Studies also indicate that the ability to work more in line with biological clocks is a significant advantage to some: there really are individuals who work best at 3am, and those people will be less stressed, and therefore take less sick leave, under flexible working conditions.

Disaster recovery

A flexible working implementation can provide, with only marginal extra cost, the basis of an organisation that would be sustainable should the use of a headquarters building, or an important satellite site, be lost owing to some unforeseen disaster (fire, flood etc), or through a terrorist incident (for example the Baltic Exchange bomb). Such incidents may still cut communications and deny access for long periods of time, even when the trigger event is at some distance and is not in any way related to the business.

Reduction of working hours lost to commuting

When employees do not have to commute every day there are less working hours spent in traffic: according to the US Federal

Highway Administration, traffic congestion is projected to cost American businesses $54 billion in lost productivity by the year 2005. Possibly even more important, however, is the reluctance of commuting staff to miss their 'good' train home, and so to cut off their work activity at often quite inappropriate and inefficient moments. Effectively, travelling time is often indistinguishable from working time for commuters: indeed many would possibly prefer to work that extra time rather than waste it travelling. Ultimately, avoiding commuting tends towards increased productivity — with increased motivation and with more hours spent working, employees are enabled to become more productive. Productivity gain is, again and again, the key benefit identified by experienced implementors of flexible working: the 1995 *TELDET* study for the EC identifies productivity gain very clearly as the single most valuable perceived benefit.[3]

Strikes affecting commuters (especially rail strikes) are a strong trigger incentive for the move to flexible working. The 1994 UK rail strikes were estimated to have cost member companies of the Institute of Directors a total of £16 million per working day (and, incidentally, quadrupled the rate of sales of notebook PCs, as businesses were forced to move over to flexible working). Quantifying the reduction in working hours lost to commuting as an annual saving is difficult but it will often be in excess of £500 per employee per annum; and in extreme cases may be ten times that.

Example 2.6.

Lombard North Central, a UK secondary bank, found from monitoring their teleworkers for two years that sick leave halved. This occurred in a group of already well-motivated people who in any case, as members of the core team, took less than half the (1991) 13 days national average sick leave. In 1993 the UK average was reported by the Trades Union Congress as having fallen to 8 days per working person, or some 1400 million hours nationally. An average 500-person office suffers a loss of 32,000 hours through sickness a year. This level of central office sick leave costs £1.34m a year in lost output per 500 people. The saving by teleworking all 500 employees would be half this figure or just under £0.7m per annum.

The **saving** per head per annum here is **£1400**

Audit of impacts

Among the items that will need to be assessed when creating the business case for flexible working there will be many that simply do not apply for any given company (not all businesses, for example, would see disaster recovery as a significant benefit — rightly or wrongly). The following checklist will help to identify those items needing further assessment in any specific case.

Audit of impacts

Major items	**Applicable?**	
Heading	**Yes**	**No**
Office space usage	❑	❑
Car park usage	❑	❑
Other office costs	❑	❑
Working capital released	❑	❑
Better staff retention	❑	❑
Reduced sick leave	❑	❑
Disaster recovery potential	❑	❑
Reduction in time lost to commuting	❑	❑

There are, of course, numerous other potential benefits that might reasonably be considered thus:

Audit of impacts

Minor items	**Applicable?**	
Heading	**Yes**	**No**
Reduced energy costs per capita	❑	❑
Reduced environmental damage	❑	❑

Reduced long distance journeys/costs	❑	❑
Reduced local journeys/costs	❑	❑
Reductions in salaries and expenses	❑	❑
Tax advantages for staff	❑	❑
Better quality of deliverable outputs	❑	❑
Greater quantity of deliverable outputs	❑	❑
Higher morale	❑	❑
Retention of staff with young children	❑	❑

An American example

Table 2.1 (from *Telecommuting*[4]) is based on work by Fleming Ltd for the State of California and shows order-of-cost saving figures broadly similar in overall scale to those discussed previously.

Table 2.1 *Benefits of telecommuting to US employers*

Personnel factors	**Benefit-savings**
Productivity (quantity)	$3000
Productivity (quality)	$1000
Recruiting and training	$1000
Retention/absenteeism	$1000
Facilities	
Office space	$1800
Parking	$200
Annual total per employee	$8000

It is worth remembering at this stage that what is being considered in this chapter is only the preparation of the business case for implementation: much of the fine detail of a scheme will remain to be assessed during a pilot implementation (see Chapter 8) and may well not be quantifiable at this stage.

Presenting the business case

Of the various potential benefits described under 'Direct financial benefits' and 'Indirect financial benefits' above, it is probable that only one or two will provide the main motivation for any given company to take action. Identifying and highlighting specific key benefits, and focusing clearly on only one or two of them, is a major factor in making a good presentation of the business case. This might be done in an executive summary (Example 2.7) accompanying a more detailed description of the pilot (Example 2.8); a budget for the costs and savings arising (Example 2.9); and a timetable (Example 2.10).

Example 2.7 Sample executive summary

X, Y and Z Order Processing Department
Flexible Working Pilot
Executive Summary

This proposal is for the introduction of flexible working into the order processing department of X, Y and Z Ltd. The costings and programmes are based on a pilot group of ten individuals, which is a large enough number to yield meaningful results without being so large as to disrupt the work, in this case order processing, during the transfer to flexible working. The order processing department has been chosen for the pilot because its tasks are well suited to being carried out remotely and being audited rather than supervised.

The objective is to achieve direct costs savings of £2500 per employee per annum in this department, while achieving simultaneously a productivity increase of 12 per cent. In total this would be equivalent to a 'saving' of £6500 per employee per annum.

The costs arising in the pilot are budgeted at £78,000, achieving a payback period of 14.4 months. This summary is accompanied by a description of the scheme, a detailed audit of the benefits and disadvantages arising, a costs budget and an implementation timetable. Permission is sought to implement the scheme by proceeding to identify tasks, individuals, locations, equipment and training needs in detail; and approval is sought for the budgeted costs.

Example 2.8 Sample description of the pilot scheme

X, Y and Z Order Processing Department
Flexible Working Pilot
Description of the Pilot Scheme

This flexible working pilot project is geared at assessing the impact and applicability of flexible working within X, Y and Z Ltd.

It is proposed to implement the pilot within the order processing department: there is scope for 38 office workstations to be relocated to the personnel's respective homes in this department alone, with a further ten being retained on-site to provide flexibility and extra cover during holidays, sickness and so on. A core team of seven would then still be maintained centrally in the existing premises, both for answering calls and for training purposes. During the 12 months pilot period only an initial ten workstations will be relocated for trial purposes, and overall staffing levels will not be affected at this stage.

The equipment to be used for each workstation will be a business telephone line, a phone, a fax machine and a modem: plus a PC with the appropriate software and a laser printer. All necessary software is already licensed to X, Y and Z, and those existing licences relate only to total numbers of users (which are unchanged) and not to their physical location. Managers within order processing have confirmed that teleworking is compatible with the way they operate, and that they expect an improvement in the quality of output from teleworkers. They also think that their office-based people and their home-based people will operate effectively together as a team. Discussions at an informal level with the relevant trade union representatives indicate agreement to the pilot provided only that it is an 'improvement only' basis, ie no loss of rights, status etc for staff involved. This is an attainable objective.

Productivity benefits will come about as a result of more flexible working patterns and of the reduction in distractions, which will enable the staff involved to cope with overloads more readily (currently overload cover is achieved by working longer hours, sometimes over weekends, with time-off in lieu being taken later).

Performance measures anticipate an average increase in productivity of around 15 per cent. Sick leave for minor illnesses is expected to reduce by about 30 per cent, based on published figures from comparable situations.

During the trial, monitoring of personnel attitudes will be undertaken to ensure that individuals are happy with flexible working and that they do actually enjoy the personal benefits resulting from flexible working hours and reduced commuting. The quality management department will use the pilot to help develop audit techniques more specifically appropriate to dispersed working, and have indicated that they support the pilot fully. Some additional load will inevitably fall on the human resource department but this is attainable within its existing programme and staffing.

Example 2.9 Sample budget: costs and savings

X, Y and Z Order Processing Department
Flexible Working Pilot
Costs and Savings

Section 1 — Extra Costs Arising (10 staff)

Additional workstations:

A	10 at £2500 each (note: but written off over two years)	£25,000
B	Use of home as office allowance — £250 × 10	£2500
C	In-home modifications (furniture, extra lines)	£5000
D	Extra management time say 200 hours @ £40	£8000
E	Modifications to network software (including staff time at £32 per hour)	£10,000
F	Cost of communications between office and home based staff (both directions)	£7500
G	Additional training and course fees	£15,000
H	Cost production time say 150 hours at £30	£4500
	Total cost	£77,500

Section 2 — savings arising (10 staff)

A	Savings in floor space 10 workplaces x 100 sq ft × £19/sq ft paid	£19,000
B	Parking costs saving 20% of the above	£3800
C	Saving on maintenance, cleaning etc pro rata 10 × £1375	£13,750
D	Productivity gain at 13% output per capita, using 1995 output values	£30,000
	Annual saving	£66,450

Section 3 — effect over 5 years (zero inflation)

1A	25,000	×1	25,000
1B	2500	×5	12,500
1C	5000	×1	5000
1D	8000	×1	8000
1E	10,000	×1	10,000
1F	7500	×5	37,500
1G	15,000	×5	75,000
1H	4500	×1	4500
5 year total cost			177,500
2A	19,000	×5	85,000
2B	3800	×5	19,000
2C	13,750	x5	68,750
2D	30,000	x5	150,000
5-year total saving			342,750
Net 5-year saving			165,250
Saving per annum per employee			£11,020

Where do we go next?

Assuming that it is clear that benefits will arise to a business, ie that a good business case for flexible working can be made, then the next step can be considered in the progress that runs thus:

- understand flexible working in outline (Chapter 1);
- make the business case (this chapter);
- prepare for trial implementation (Chapters 3–7);
- implement a flexible working trial (Chapter 8);
- become a flexible working business (Chapter 9).

The next five chapters deal with the various prerequisites to creating a successful trial implementation: without full preparation a trial is likely either to fail or to be inconclusive, so preparation matters.

Example 2.10 Sample implementation timetable

X, Y and Z Order Processing Department
Flexible Working Pilot
Implementation Timetable

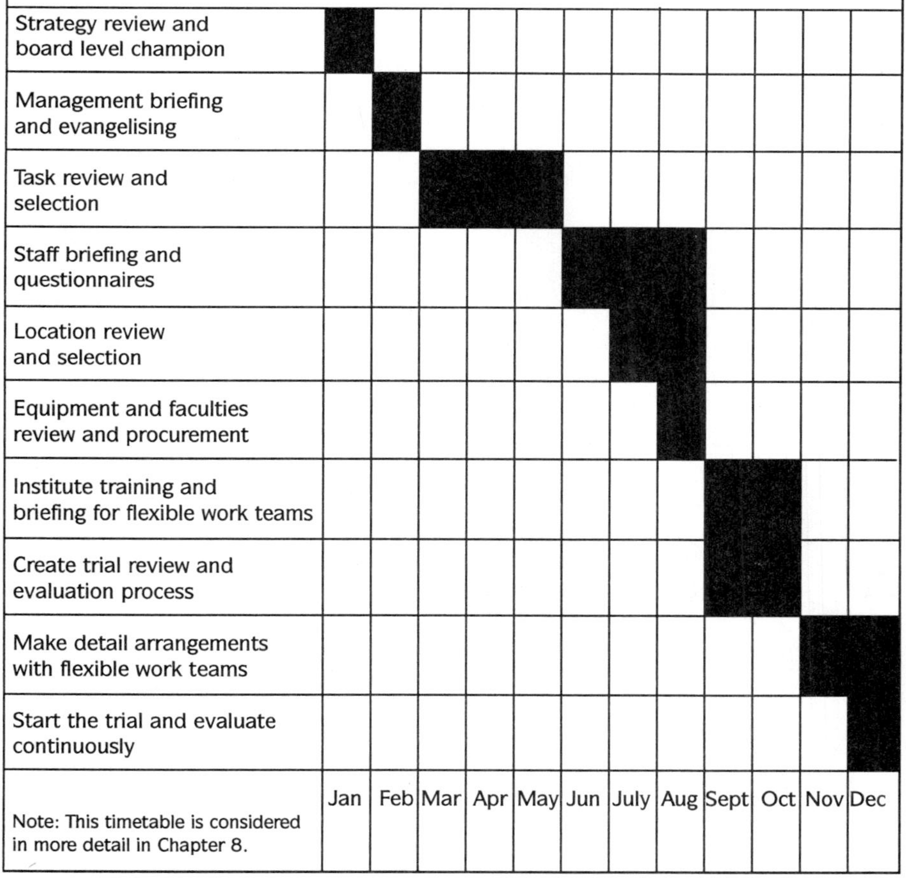

Chapter 3

Choosing tasks for flexible working

Choosing the general field

For many businesses, the choice of general fields of work within which to consider flexible working is, initially at least, glaringly obvious. In many cases, even prior to considering a formal flexible working pilot, there will have been an informal, tacit, spread of flexible working. This will often have been associated with some 'exceptional' circumstances, for instance:

- to cope with the exceptional demands of a large and urgent project;
- to delay moving to larger premises, or to achieve a smooth transfer to new premises;
- to keep closer to a major client, or to a newly acquired client;
- to retain skilled staff (particularly key staff just starting families), and also individuals with health problems who are happy to work at home but cannot cope with the greater stresses of commuting or the office.

The 'exceptional' circumstances will, in fact, occur all the time and flexible working may well already be widely accepted.

Such instances of 'tacit' flexible working would naturally influence the choice of general fields of work very substantially: building on what exists already often will be easier than starting afresh, so creating a first formal implementation around an informal, tacit, existing implementation, will often be a favoured choice. However, where it is the case that flexible working is to be considered from a cold start, and where there is no immediate obvious field to consider, then looking at what other businesses have already done may be helpful. The questions here are obviously:

- Do other companies like ours implement flexible working?
- What fields have they introduced flexible working in?

Types of business that can benefit (classified by size)

As discussed in Chapter 1 there are some interesting features to be found in the research figures relating to the sizes of organisations already involved in flexible working (Table 3.1).

Table 3.1 *Occurrences of organisations involved in flexible working*

Number of employees	Occurrences of flexible working (%)
1000 plus	28
500–999	11
100–499	28
50–99	2
1–49	31

Source: EC *TELDET* project.[1]

What is most interesting here is the 'hole in the middle' effect, which can be highlighted by summarising the figures, as in Table 3.2.

Table 3.2 *The 'hole in the middle' effect*

Number of employees	Occurrences of flexible working (%)
More than 100	67
50–99	2
1–49	31

Businesses that already benefit from flexible working are thus virtually all sizes of businesses: in practice, however, it seems that companies in or about the size range of say 20–99 employees find it most disruptive to implement formal flexible working. That may be because, on the one hand, they lack the larger overhead budgets of bigger corporates and therefore do not have data processing managers or in-house information technology (IT) or local area network (LAN) managers to sort out their technology. On the other hand, they may be too large already for the principals or directors of the business to be involved in implementing flexible working personally. This clearly raises a question mark against flexible working implementation for such small to middle-sized businesses. Even allowing for that one specific potential difficulty, however, there still remain about 90 per cent of all businesses that can potentially benefit, particularly those with significant service elements. As technology implementations become more and more commonplace the 'hole in the middle' effect becomes slighter and slighter. Figure 3.1 identifies the main sectors of business contained within Tables 3.1 and 3.2.

Types of business that can benefit (classified by industry)

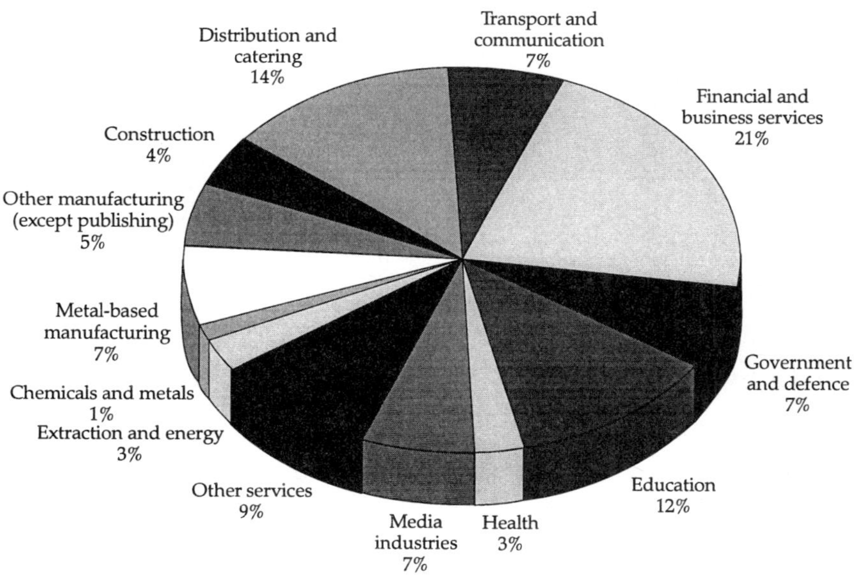

Figure 3.1 *Industry sectors contained within Tables 3.1 and 3.2*

Types of business that can benefit (classified by tasks)

Flexible working is still in a phase of rapid development: new sectors are still being developed and will be for many years yet. In general, however, the outlines of what constitute suitable sectors for flexible working are very clear. Two other surveys, one for the EC (Figure 3.2) and one for the UK Department of Employment (Figure 3.3.), show patterns of diffusion by tasks undertaken. However, it is not possible to define these very precisely because of the difficulty of describing tasks uniquely, and the lack of commonly accepted terminology for description.

Based on the following figures, the Department of Employment in its *A Manager's Guide to Teleworking*[4] suggests the following occupations as being suited to flexible working:

The most usual flexible work occupations are:

- management;
- sales and marketing;
- computer programming;
- other IT specialisms;
- consultancy;
- training and education;
- writing and editing;
- research;
- secretarial work;
- administration;
- data entry and typing.

Flexible work also may be suitable for:

- translators;
- designers;
- planners;
- social workers;
- telephone counsellors;
- inspectors;
- legal workers;
- accountants;
- financial advisers;
- engineers;

and many other occupations.

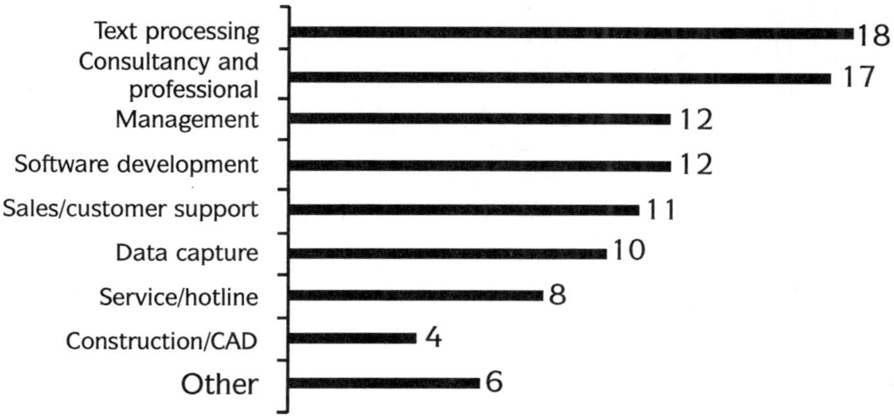

Figure 3.2 *Flexible working tasks — EC statistics*

Base: 78 companies expressed as a percentage.
Source: *European Telecommunications Handbook for Teleworkers.*[2]

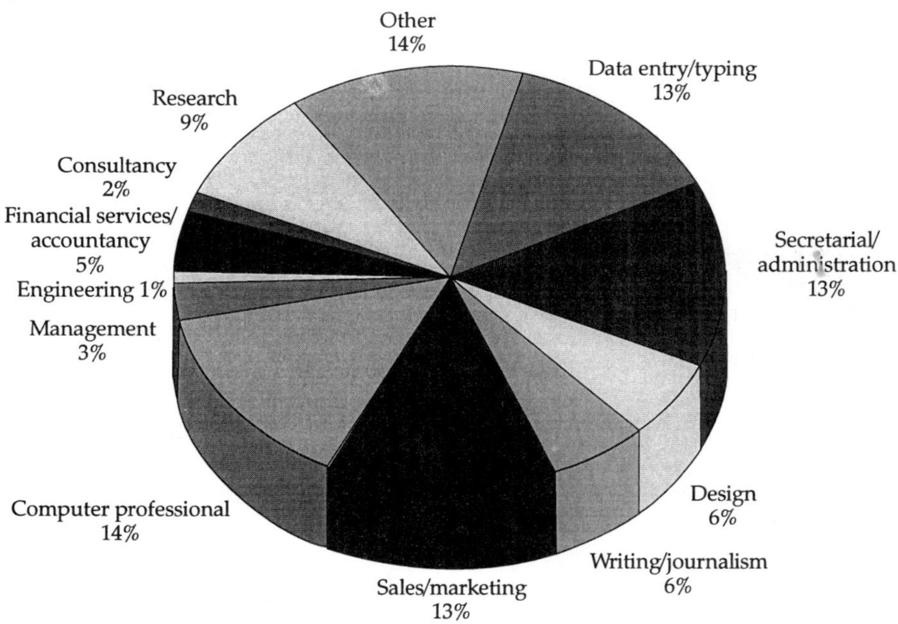

Figure 3.3 *Flexible working tasks — UK statistics*

Source: Department of Employment.[3]

Defining tasks more precisely

Assuming that there is a prima facie business case that flexible working might be appropriate for your business (Chapter 2), the practicality is that some specific tasks have to be chosen for a 'pilot' implementation, and that will necessitate identifying the workgroup to be involved both in terms of people (Chapter 4) and in terms of the specific tasks.

Principles for choosing tasks

Ideally tasks should be:

- information based, not physical product based;
- learly definable in output terms (eg targets);
- clearly definable in programme terms (eg milestones);
- capable of communication as either voice or data (ie telecommunicable).

Obviously the 'information-based' nature of tasks has led historically to a preponderance of IT tasks in flexible work but this is slowly being worked through: a survey for the NCC[5] found actual tasks to be those shown in Table 3.3.

Table 3.3 *Tasks in flexible working*

Type of job	Numbers reported	Time at home (%)	No. of organisations
IT development	316	74	28
IT support	25	5	4
IT management	2	6	2
IT others*	865	66	5
Sales staff	505	20	10
Sales management	51	20	5
Field engineers	160	18	2
Secretarial/administration	13	82	4
Journalists	113	90	2
Bankers	200	20	1
Consultants	1	50	1
Education advisers	405	15	2
Research scientists	9	25	2
Training co-ordinators	2	20	1
Investment analysts	4	25	1
Life consultants	5	na	1
Customer relations	50	25	1

Managers (not specified)	78	16	4
Project managers	4	25	1
Others (not specified)	9	48	2

*Includes 800 workers on unspecified activities at one particular IT company.

One of the most important factors in the choice of tasks is the ability to define outputs (preferably in some quantified way) and thus to create programmes and budgets that are, and remain, meaningful. This is the factor that builds confidence in senior management and, more important, allows line management to feel that they are not risking their careers on a dream that cannot be fulfilled: those considerations are vital in practice, if schemes are to be implemented correctly without unnecessary obstacles.

Job analysis audit

Size of business	**Positive**	**Negative**
1–49 employees	❑	
50–99 employees		❑
More than 100 employees	❑	

If positive, go on to the next section (Industry sectors).

If negative, check out the section 'Types of business that can benefit' before proceeding.

Industry sectors

Does the business have an involvement in:

Financial services	❑
Business services	❑
Information technology	❑
Publishing	❑
Education	❑
Media industries and publishing	❑
Transport and distribution	❑
Communications	❑

Design and manufacturing ❑

Health ❑

If one or more of these sectors is applicable, go on to the next section,

otherwise reconsider the section 'Types of business that can benefit'.

Tasks

Does the business have substantial activities in:

Text processing ❑

Consultancy and professional work ❑

Management ❑

Software development ❑

Sales and customer liaison ❑

Data capture/databasing ❑

Customer service/support hotline ❑

CAD/CAM ❑

By this stage the choice of task area should be apparent.

Other criteria

At this stage it is likely to be apparent that there are fields of activity in the business that offer the potential for flexible working: however, choosing specific tasks for flexible working implementation will involve other considerations than just their theoretical suitability for the purpose. Among the other factors to be considered there are questions relating to:

Scale — How many individuals do we wish to use for a pilot?

Departments — Can a suitable number be assembled in a coherent group, ie in only a small number of different departments?

Risk levels	Can a group be established to undertake a pilot without causing risk to a specific project or department through 'taking the eye off the ball'?
Demand	Is there evidence of employee-led demand for flexible working in a particular department? *Note*: the evidence here may be implicit, eg high absenteeism perhaps, or exceptional vulnerability to disruption by rail strikes.
Implementation	Are there existing groups working in a tacit flexible working manner, eg separating working at home for peace and quiet from their office teamwork role ?
Loners	Are there some individuals whose work is substantially detached from office routine, eg technical authors, journalists, consultants etc?
Staying in touch	Are there individuals who have to be constantly on call (to customers, but also possibly to secretaries or to the board)?
Supporters	Are there individuals whose activities are essentially a support function (not just desktop PC support but also engineering support, design advice and such like)?

Job analysis in detail

Specific tasks, existing and re-engineered

One of the side-effects of the introduction of flexible working to an organisation is that it casts new light on existing practices: having located a group of individuals handling tasks well suited to flexible working, then the next activity should be to pull off the shelf the job descriptions and procedures that relate to those tasks. Very often these will not exist, of course: it will probably therefore be necessary to create them at this stage. Given that job analysis and process analysis are very time consuming tasks, and thus represent a very substantial investment, there will be a natural tendency at this stage to jump straight to a new, idealised, re-engineered flexible work situation in which the flexible working pilot also addresses existing weaknesses in organisation and ways of working. The introduction of flexible working can legitimately be seen as a trigger for business process re-engineering (BPRE), and often will be a part of BPRE implementation, so it would be naive to say that the focus of a flexible working pilot should not be blurred by excessive re-engineering at the outset. However, it is generally the case that evolution works better than revolution in this area: flexible working implementation is clearly more likely to achieve its initial goals if those goals are restricted to eg cost savings or productivity gains. If they include wider BPRE objectives, then there will be an increased risk of failure arising from the potential loss of focus.

Where there seems to be an overlap between flexible working pilots and BPRE pilots (which will be frequent), Chapters 5, 6 and 7 of *Business Process Re-Engineering — Myth and Reality*[6] are essential reading.

The following extract from that reference summarises the implications of BPRE for flexible working implementation. It was written by Simon Robinson of Empirica, author also of reference 1 in Chapter 1 of this book.

- Horizontal compression of whole processes into the job of a single case-teleworker weakens or removes any requirement on telework managers for ongoing monitoring of results.
- Vertical compression, moving decision making down the hierarchy, means that the front line teleworker rarely has to refer to the manager for authorisation and further relieves telework managers.
- Accelerating processes by removing unnecessary sequentiality constraints reduces the overhead for chasing late orders etc.
- Burdening front-line teleworkers with the decision as to whether a given case of work is simple enough for them to handle alone may increase management overhead unless adequate software support for these decisions is provided.
- Moving work 'to where it makes most sense' generally brings with it an increased sophistication of telework jobs, and a reduction of the need for co-ordination by telework management.
- Introducing *statistical* rather than *continuous* monitoring and checking can greatly reduce some of the problems found in traditional telework management.
- Supporting team self-management in telework, ie without team co-location, means careful consideration of commu-

nication support between team-members: support must have very low threshold and disturbance, at best better than communication opportunities in co-location.

- Multidimensional telework jobs requires careful management at its introduction rather than day-to-day, and raises the skill requirements of both teleworkers and their managers.
- Empowerment and the responsibility devolvement it implies relieves management of much control work, and makes management of telework less different from management of on-site staff.
- Encouraging and arranging for life-long education of the telework-force is a growing challenge not only in telework management.
- Removing the need for reconciliation of documents originating from different domains (of consistency control) and avoiding any need for such reconciliation between teleworker and employer can greatly reduce overhead work and its management.
- Where teleworkers are managers and provide a point of contact to their employer's customers, this may limit the freedom of self-selection of working time, which is in many cases a major motivator to take up telework.
- Centralising automated control while increasing decentralised autonomy increases the viability of teleworking and relieves telework management of another burden.
- Moving the basis of compensation from activity or time to results, potentially gives rise to the management task of intermediate outcome evaluation and associated negotiation. The simultaneous integration across the length of a process removes this overhead again.
- Identifying candidates for a change of post should be decoupled from performance monitoring, using techniques such as assessment centres for both teleworkers and other candidates, including external applicants.
- Introducing re-engineered values significantly reduces a need for motivating or driving activity by telework managers.

- Telework managers are not automatically to be recruited from good team performers, but rather to be chosen for their coaching and enabling skills.
- In an organisation structured as 'a bunch of co-equals just doing work', coaching ratios of over 1 to 20 will be common, with a consequential decrease in the number of telework managers, but raising issues of providing communication channels between coach and a large telework team.

In conclusion, management functions in a re-engineered working environment are less extensive on most counts than in traditional organisations. The management role is more nearly equal between on-site and teleworking staff, but requirements for sophisticated communication and decision support are significantly greater.

Specific tasks, quality management

Procedures prepared under BS 5750 or ISO 900*x* standards also make valuable bases for flexible working job activities: writing these procedures is a less daunting task than is the job and process analysis for BPRE. See Chapter 7 for more information about quality management in flexible working.

Summary

The outcome at this stage should be:

- A decision on the appropriate number of individuals to be moved to flexible working (eg 12).
- A decision on the departmental location or locations of these tasks (eg customer support).
- First indications of any employee-led demand for flexible work in these areas, explicitly but also implicitly (eg deduced from absenteeism rates).
- First indications of any specific individuals who may be tacit flexible workers.

- Some indication of the intention to attempt simultaneous process re-engineering (but see the warning in 'Specific tasks, existing and re-engineered' above).

Things to be avoided as outcomes are:

- Individuals making unwarranted deductions that they will necessarily be involved in subsequent actions.
- Large re-engineering implications accidentally triggered by small flexible working intentions.
- Fears of redundancy, loss of status, disruption etc.

Means of dealing with the first and last of these risks are discussed in Chapter 4.

Chapter 4

Choosing people for flexible working

Selecting people

A commonly quoted rule of thumb for personnel selection for flexible working is that three volunteers are required for interview (or personality profiling or whatever other process is used) for each one eventually selected. Given that the necessary task selection has been carried out (see Chapter 3) and that the proposed job content is therefore fairly well defined, it is necessary to look next at personal characteristics and relationships with others in the business. People questions are also involved in training (see Chapter 7); equipment (see Chapter 6); and considerations of location and working conditions (see Chapter 5).

Personal characteristics

The academic view

Celia and John Stanworth who have made a speciality of examining personnel issues in flexible working, writing in *The European Journal of Teleworking*,[1] looked at the personal characteristics needed to make a good (and happy) flexible worker (Figure 4.1).

Within the personal characteristics that flexible workers considered important shown in Figure 4.1, the essentials of independence — the need for self-discipline and the ability to 'self-start' — emerge strongly. Many flexible workers feel that the type of personality embracing these traits is certainly not universally distributed and may well be confined to only a relatively small minority of the population, particularly in respect of self-motivation and the ability to organise time. This, however, is not yet proven and may just be an elitist viewpoint corresponding to the early stage of development of flexible work.

A particular finding of the Stanworths' study was the way in which flexible workers may develop elaborate patterns of almost ritualistic behaviour in order to build structure and discipline into their work lives. The latter are sometimes combined with another of the needs which features strongly in Figure 4.1, that is the need to separate work and home life. For, as the Stanworths express it, whereas some people find it possible to begin work at irregular times, possibly still dressed in their pyjamas and dressing gown, others prefer the practice of a disciplined break. Hence, it is not unknown for people to even 'dress for work' at the exact same time each day, much as they would do for the office and, in some cases, to even leave the house and walk around the block before letting themselves back into the house and, 'on arrival', begin work. For these people, other aspects of the day's work are equally likely to be punctuated with structure and routine. For instance, the timing of tea, coffee and lunch breaks may be highly routinised, to the greatest extent that the turbulence of a normal working day is likely to allow. Almost identical findings were reported by Leslie Haddon in 'Teleworking in the 1990s — A View from the Home'.[2] Haddon's department at the University of Sussex has specialised in tracking opinions and attitudes among those working at home over long periods of time.

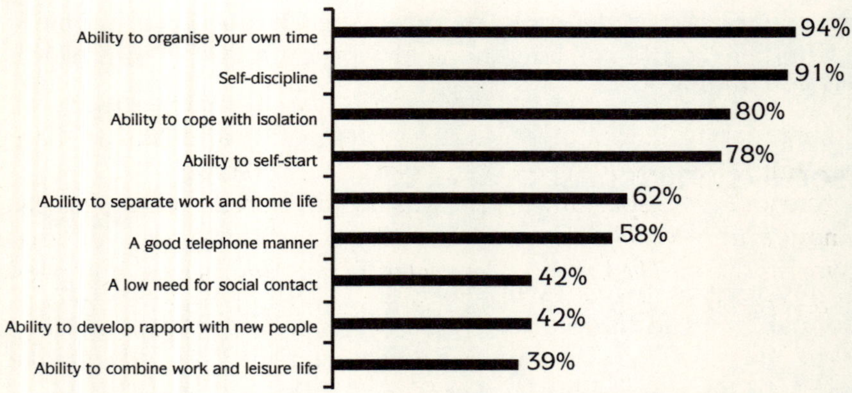

Figure 4.1 *What personal characteristics do you need?*

Source: *The European Journal of Teleworking*[1]; from a sample of 371 respondents.

Returning to Figure 4.1 once again, it can be seen that, while the ability to cope with isolation and the reduced stress levels of social contact emerges strongly, the need for social skills was also stressed by around half of a sample of 371 respondents, and that figure rose to 58 per cent in the case of crucial telephone skills. Also, the need to develop rapport with new people was stressed, since in-house project managers often come and go, requiring the forging and development of new relationships with the new managers who 'inherit' the existing flexible work teams.

The company view

Both the Department of Employment, and Mercury Communications have also listed the personality characteristics required for teleworking in broadly similar ways to those identified by Leslie Haddon and by the Stanworths. First, the Department of Employment, in *A Manager's Guide to Teleworking*[3] suggests as the main requirements:

- Maturity.
- Trustworthiness.
- Self-sufficiency.
- Self-discipline.
- Good time management skills.
- Good communication skills.

In fact, maturity and trustworthiness seem merely to be icons of desirability here, rather than to have any specific quality attached to them. Assuming, however, that the missing hyphen comes after, rather than before, 'time', the rest of the list seems like common sense .

Mercury's corresponding list was co-authored with Francis Kinsman, author of *The Telecommuters* (Penguin Books) and, like the Stanworths' list in *The European Journal of Teleworking*, is based on personal responses (and benefits from being prioritised). In order of priority, the characteristics described (mostly unprompted) by his respondents were:

- Self-discipline — a self-starter.
- Well-organised in time management.
- Dedicated.
- Able to work on one's own.
- Confident — prepared to ask for help.

- A good communicator.
- Flexibility and adaptability.
- Technical experience.
- Trustworthiness.
- Psychological stability.

Source: *The Flexible Working Portfolio.*[4]

From these opinions one might reasonably distil a set of priorities thus:

Priority number 1:	Time management.
	Self-discipline and good time-management.
Priority number 2:	Motivation management.
	Self-sufficiency, self-starting, ability to work alone.
Priority number 3:	Communication management.
	Good communication skills, good telephone manner, ability to get on with new people.
Priority number 4:	Lifestyle management.
	Ability to manage the split between home life, working life and leisure and to manage social contacts.
Priority number 5:	Technology management. Ability to cope with equipment.

It is interesting to observe that this is a very similar list to what might be proposed as the desirable characteristics for the management team for a start-up new business: flexible work does indeed make 'employees' look much more like 'entrepreneurs' in many ways. In the context of selecting teams it is important to realise that long-term employees who have become 'institutionalised' may not be happy to lose the crutch of accustomed support.

This point is reflected in a different way by looking at the age profiles of teleworkers (see Bailyn[5]): very few are under age 25 and it is easy to speculate that the attraction of the high social content of urban office life might have most influence here. Similarly, the low numbers over age 55 might be due partly to a desire to return to a more supportive environment later in life, although the age profile in IT sectors is frequently skewed away from this age group. It is worth remembering, however, that individuals change during their lives: flexible working must have the flexibility to support both office environments and telework environments equally and to allow the move from one to another as individual perceptions and needs change.

Accommodating the changing perceptions of individuals is indeed a major factor in achieving success: the perceptions of existing flexible workers, as itemised by the Stanworths, gives clear indicators of the factors involved in the choice of a flexible working team (Figure 4.2).

Social drawbacks

Particularly where flexible work involves some element of working at home, there may be questions to be addressed in the impact on home life: as a generality, flexible workers tend to rate the increased quality of life as a major plus point of flexible working, but some difficulties can arise. Leslie Haddon writing in *The European Journal of Teleworking*[2] said that:

> Some flexible working employees have to co-ordinate their activities with others who are still working core hours in an office. Both flexible working employees and the flexible working self-employed also need to be contactable at certain times. Case studies reveal instances of managers regularly having to face crises at times not of their own choosing, and of both clerical and professional self-employed flexible workers working longer hours than they would like because of rush jobs, the need to bring new products to market, consultancy deadlines, or short-term notice of work.
>
> At the same time, flexible workers often experience pressures to synchronise their non-working lives with others both inside and outside the home. Female clerical workers, as well as some professionals, who cannot afford to pay for childcare can often only work when the children are not around or when their partners can look after them. In cases where young children are present in the home, this means that the only practical time to work is in the evenings and at weekends. Or some flexible workers try to keep weekends free to retain a place in the community — since that is when social activities are most likely to occur.

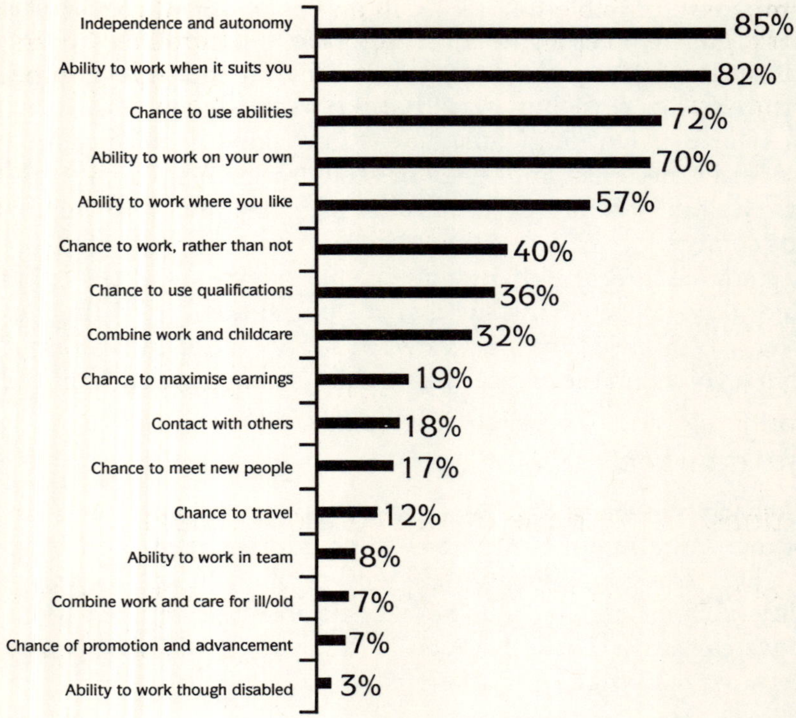

Figure 4.2 *Which of the above do you think your present job gives you?*

Source: *The European Journal of Teleworking.*[1]

Social constraints also affect the location of flexible work. Although regular commitments to visit one or more worksites may limit flexible workers' choice of where they would want to live, of far more significance is domestic inertia. Houses are still hard to sell in the UK housing market. People are part of communities. Their children have friends at local schools. And they usually have partners whose own work commitments and preferences have to be considered. On the whole, flexibility does not lead people radically to relocate and decamp to the countryside. Within the home, impression management can be a significant issue for flexible workers. They can feel that they are not seen as really working simply because they are not going out to work. Some men feel they might be perceived as being unemployed, some women that their working being seen as mere pin money when in fact their income made a significant contribution to household funds. Moreover, most are keen to create the right image for employers or clients: as being professional,

> competent and able to operate in an environment convivial to work. Hence, keeping order in the house, controlling extraneous noises (eg from children) and in some cases displaying their technology became important impression management issues.

These issues need to be aired at the time when people are being selected: in practice, it is very difficult to make selection criteria to cover them and they are more likely to be addressed in, rather than prior to, a trial. However, the earlier they are raised the more likely a satisfactory resolution becomes. It is also worth noting that the context in which Haddon made these remarks was that of surveying social drawbacks: they are not intended to represent an even handed evaluation of the value of working from home, but do have value as a prior warning of possible adverse effects on personnel.

Relationships with the team and the business

Most of this chapter has been concerned with how flexible working affects people: there is, however, also a consideration of how the choice of people for flexible working may impact on the business (ie a wider question than that of efficiency or inefficiency).

Bailyn[5] identified a personality trait in self-selected flexible workers, in which the wellbeing of the task (contract, project etc) becomes more important than the wellbeing of the business. This effect is common enough in any business, and is healthy where people merely fight their corner for a department, contract or project. However, flexible workers can potentially become sufficiently detached from a business to lose all sense of proportion, and then put in far more effort and far more time than a particular job warrants in a search for perfection that fulfils their self-image in respect of the 'job', as a substitute for the drip-feed of self-fulfilment that used to come in respect of the business as a whole. Focus can be valuable, but flexible working can convert it to obsession: consequently, potentially obsessive individuals need particularly careful management in flexible working.

The second major factor in the relationship between choice of people for flexible working and the health of the business, is the potential to truncate career progression through individuals becoming 'lost to sight' in a flexible working implementation. In this respect flexible working must genuinely be seen to be a part of the standard career progression, or otherwise the most ambitious people will shun it. Allowing a flexible working implementation to become a self selection of the self-effacing and unambitious will inevitably impact badly on its outcome, as well as on the individuals concerned.

Selecting the people

Warming up

Prior to any specific action in selection, it will be necessary to circulate a brief description of the proposed pilot, some information about flexible working (possibly by using copies of suppliers' (eg BT or Mercury) publications), and some outline guidance on the criteria that would tend to make individuals opt for flexible working. It is vital to establish at this stage that there will be

- no compulsion;
- no loss of earnings;
- no loss of pension;
- no loss of status;
- no loss of career prospects;
- full ability to revert to office-based employment.

In this respect Appendix A offers some useful views from the trade union standpoint: businesses considering outsourcing may need to refer to the Transfer of Undertakings (Protection of Employment) Regulations of 1981 — see Chapter 5, 'Effective dismissal and TUPER'.

Asking questions of staff

Asking questions 'involves' people and makes them feel a part of the scheme from the outset: to encourage this feeling, each set of questions should be prefaced with at least some indication of the reasoning behind the questions. Subjects on which detailed information (over and above normal personal records) will be needed include:

- Commuting patterns and attitudes.
- Space availability at home.
- Partner's opinions.
- Children's daily routines.
- Attitudes to technology.
- Attitudes to flexible working.
- Fears and concerns.

This clearly embarks on some sensitive issues, and scope must be left for questions to remain unanswered without embarrassment. If there is a trade union presence then the content of any questionnaire should be discussed in advance (see Appendix A).

Recruiting management

Notwithstanding the extreme sensitivity of some of the questions raised above, it is normally the case that the prospect of flexible working will be welcomed by staff because of its clear benefits to their quality of life. Over and over again, however, studies have shown that hostility from line management can be a major drawback in flexible working implementation. Generally speaking, the quality of life benefits will be less clear cut for management, who may see a flexible working scheme as having no upside potential for them: if it works well they foresee no credit, just more complex working patterns. If it goes badly, they expect to get the blame. Good handling of the early stages of selection of suitable managers may well be a make or break question for a flexible working implementation.

The attractive issue for managers is likely to be that of keeping up with new developments: flexible working has to be clearly identified as the shape of things to come, and a pilot or trial scheme as the opportunity to get in at the beginning. A typical 10 or 20 person pilot will need two or three enthusiastic managers to be fully committed. Given their natural career aspirations, it will also be necessary to have at least one senior manager seen to be acting as an enthusiastic champion for flexible working so that the line managers do not feel excessively exposed to status risk themselves. This involves real consideration of the politics of the situation. Chapters 8 and 9 in *Working in Organizations* by Kakabadse, Ludlow and Vinnicombe[6] would be particularly valuable reading at this stage, since a good understanding of both the power structure (championing), and the concept of stakeholders in a situation, are required if alienation is to be avoided.

Using freelance flexible workers

Flexible working tends to change the nature of the relationship between business and staff. In principle, there should be no difference in the criteria applied. However, the looser tie with freelance staff does make some revised structures advisable. A number of bodies exist concerned with freelance flexible workers: some agencies (Alfred Marks, Computer People, etc) are specialists in the field, and some associations (National Association of Teleworking, Telecottage Association, etc) support freelance flexible workers.

Codes of conduct and practice

To a degree, using freelance flexible staff can be facilitated by membership of associations (and by close ties with a reputable agency). Most such bodies call for their members to subscribe to some sort of Code: as an example, the following is the document used by Cornwall TelNet, a support operation for flexible workers in the far South West of England. This is a very simple concept to implement, requiring only agreement by all parties. Quality management achieves similar objectives more fully, but needs more training support: the topic of quality management is therefore considered in Chapter 7.

Example 4.1

Why have a code of conduct for teleworkers?

Research carried out on behalf of Devon and Cornwall Training and Enterprise Council identified that one of the main factors which was inhibiting the growth of the teleworking industry was the general lack of confidence that buyers experienced when considering making a purchase from an unknown teleworker.

In its current state the teleworking industry often lacks any form of quality assurance, beyond that which the individual teleworker brings in the form of professional or vocational qualifications and personal or business reputation.

TelNet code of conduct

In order to build purchasers' confidence in telework, there is a need for the establishment of clear working standards for teleworkers. Cornwall TelNet has developed a set of standards which are embodied in its Code of Conduct. The Code of Conduct represents the public presentation of an orderly approach to teleworking.

All teleworkers registered with Cornwall TelNet agree to work to the standards of teleworking laid down in the Code of Conduct. How the standards embodied in the Code of Conduct are achieved is up to each individual teleworker, but a Code of Practice is also provided which gives advice and guidance on the methods which could be used.

The TelNet Code of Conduct

- To carry out the assignment which the teleworker has undertaken diligently, conscientiously and with proper regard for the client's interests.
- To apply good management and quality assurance practices to all teleworking assignments.
- To agree with the client a written statement which clearly identifies the objectives and scope of the proposed work, the timescale and fee basis, and also where necessary to agree in writing any subsequent revision.
- To respect all information concerning the client's business as strictly confidential and not to disclose or permit the disclosure of any such information without the client's specific prior permission.
- To ensure that all property, data, test and other materials belonging to the client and held by the teleworker are stored in a secure location when not in use and handled appropriately when in use.
- To only accept such assignments for which the teleworker is suitably qualified and/or experienced to carry out to a high standard.
- To refrain from undertaking any assignment which would result in a conflict of interest and to disclose to the client any financial or personal interest which may influence the work carried out for the client in any way.
- To ensure that all hardware and software used by the teleworker is used only in connection with the teleworker's professional activities, is properly maintained and that all reasonable care is taken to ensure that it is free from defects.
- To ensure that the teleworker's knowledge and skills are kept up to date, where necessary through obtaining appropriate training and professional development.

Code of Practice

While the Code of Conduct is a public expression of the standards within which a teleworker undertakes to work, it gives no actual guidance to the teleworker on how to achieve the desired result. This guidance is provided by the Code of Practice, which is divided into three sections. The first section deals with ethical considerations, the second section covers contractual arrangements, while the third section provides details of procedures and practices.

Ethical

Purchasers of teleworking products and services must by necessity, place a high degree of trust in the individual teleworker. It is important therefore that customers are assured that as a teleworker, you will carry out your work in a proper and ethical manner. Security and confidentiality are the areas in which customers are likely to be most concerned. They will also need to be assured that you will carry out your work for them with due diligence.

Contractual

Contracts

All telework carried out under the Code of Conduct will be supported by written agreement between purchaser and supplier. Such an agreement or contract should cover the following minimum points:

- The identities and contact addresses of both purchaser and supplier and, where either is a corporate body, the names of the individuals concerned.
- A general description of the work to be carried out, and its purpose and scope.
- The payment to be made for the work, including where appropriate a statement that VAT will be applicable.
- A timetable for both the work and payment for it.
- A clear description of the proposals for confidentiality and security of the work and its Data Protection Act status.

- A definition of the ownership of any resulting copyright and intellectual property rights.
- Arrangements for loan/supply of equipment where applicable including insurance arrangements.
- Arrangements in the event of illness, incapacity, holidays etc and for consequent subcontracting if permitted.
- Where the work load exceeds 21 hours per week and is an exclusive use of the teleworker full-time, arrangements for PAYE and NI deductions (in these circumstances the teleworker is likely to be classified as an employee for the duration of the work).
- Where group working is involved, the identity of the individual responsible for quality within the group.

NB Where the work proposed is of limited extent then the items listed above may be very brief: all should, however, always be present in some clear form even if they are very brief.

NB Registered teleworkers will normally carry out telework in accordance with all UK legal requirements. Contracts and agreements will be interpreted accordingly.

Appraisals and contract review

Having defined 'what is to be done' in the contract or agreement for the work, the second main part of the code relates to the important activities involved in appraising 'what has been done' and, especially, its compliance with the contract. To check compliance, groups of teleworkers would appraise one another's performance: individuals will have no option but to look formally at their own performance. Checks on quality matters in group working would normally be handled by review meeting: individuals will need to schedule specific appraisal sessions for the same purpose. In what follows the terms 'review meetings' and 'appraisal sessions' are interchangeable.

Running an appraisal session

Regular appraisal sessions should be held at which the following items are on the agenda at appropriate intervals, and appropriate minutes are kept of the outcome.

- Task planning, task development and task management (this includes contract compliance review).
- Purchasing and or subcontracting of tasks (also including contract compliance review).
- Inspection of work.
- Corrective action.
- Training needs and status.

Appropriate intervals for these might be no less than eight times a year for the first four items, and once a year for training. Frequencies should be stated.

Record keeping

Formal record keeping is the third main aspect of the Code. Since all teleworkers will at some time be required to keep work under lock and key because its disclosure (even accidentally) is an offence under the Data Protection Act, a lockable document file will be required, containing:

- Contracts and contract documents in indexed files.
- Agenda for and minutes of appraisal sessions in sequence.
- A working diary (times, data, tasks, inspections and results, including corrective action).
- An adverse events diary, which may be included in the previous point but should be separately indexed (non-compliance, inspection failures, data losses, equipment failures, incapacity resulting in delay etc).
- Training records and results.
- Approved subcontractors list (which can be the TelNet or some similar database).
- Document log recording all the above and their issue as appropriate (eg to clients). Where these documents exist in various versions (eg contracts) a log of version number is required, and a record of the issue of each. If a document must be reissued whenever a new version comes into use, that fact should be highlighted and appropriate action noted.

- All data belonging to clients.

Measurements

As far as most teleworkers are concerned, the measurements involved in teleworking will be concerned with quantifying work carried out for the purpose of determining methods and amounts of payment.

Types of work and payment measurements

Salaried work

Where the purchaser/employer is accustomed to operating by audit of performance, rather than by supervision of activity, mere relocation of the site of work does not upset the operation of that audit, which is effectively therefore the most important means of measurement of work.

Time rates

It is important to appreciate that audit of performance (generally achieved by comparison with a notional standard) is also an essential part of time rate working. Very precise time record keeping is clearly indicated: software for time recording, allocation and charging is available for this specific purpose. The administrative load of this must fall on the teleworker and generally the teleworker will have to use IT methods to handle it adequately.

Lump sum working and piece rates

It is desirable that piece-work prices should be part of a sequence so that experience can operate to improve pricing, and so that change can operate to balance the swings and the roundabouts. Despite an often unfortunate history, piece rate working remains both common and, often, popular. Text writing (*x* per thousand words) and database entry (*x* per hundred names and addresses) are common examples. As with lump sum working, the ability to reassess the rate over a long sequence of work is a necessary precondition for success: often purchasers will have such long experience, but suppliers need to exercise normal caution over rates (and purchasers over acceptability of work).

Equipment

Where a particular teleworking task involves unusual or special equipment, the telework purchasers will normally expect to have to provide it. Where teleworkers are expected to supply their own equipment, the expectation will be for commonplace items: for example a PC (generally IBM-compatible), probably a fax machine, and always a telephone.

Teleworkers will provide a telephone and a commonplace PC at their own expense.

Technical standards

As with equipment, so with technical standards: if what is proposed is not entirely commonplace, then the purchasing client is naturally going to expect to have to provide support to the teleworker. However, good communication and understanding are at the heart of teleworking: all involved need to speak the same language. For this reason, even non-technical teleworkers are likely to need at least minimal training in the language of IT to attain a level of competence such that terms such as ASCII file, Modem, Serial and Parallel, back-up, tapestreamer, DOS, Unix and so on are understood. For non-technical teleworkers, specific training giving an overview of IT terminology is likely to be both necessary and desirable.

Training and development

Many teleworkers have general professional or technical qualifications which will be meaningful to the purchasers of their services. Many others will have specifically related vocational qualifications. In the long term it is clear that all teleworkers should ideally possess (and, equally important, maintain) recognised and relevant qualifications.

Teleworkers will need to maintain their training standard such that they are fully aware of current technical development in their field of work.

Chapter 5

Choosing locations for flexible working

Introduction

Whatever the particular flavour of a flexible working implementation, it will inevitably mean the effective physical relocation of the site of work for many of those involved, to any or all of:

- home-based offices;
- hot desking and/or satellite offices or drop-in centres;
- mobile offices in hotels, vehicles or *ad hoc* locations.

Within the conventional office-based environment, a whole raft of activities are handled as part of the general office overheads, and these costs all still apply in a flexible working environment, albeit that they may become very much less of a burden. The items include:

- premises, leases and mortgages;
- business rates and planning consents;
- insurances;
- heating and lighting;
- telephone and communications;
- health and safety;
- data security and data protection.

As the importance of premises declines, these items move from being general office overhead to being a part of the contractual relationship with members of the flexible working teams: at the same time, they may move on the accounts from being part of the fixed overhead (not dependent on sales) to part of the variable overhead (dependent on sales). (This paper movement in the accounts can be one of the main perceived benefits of flexible working as seen by financial directors.) Cost impacts for these items are discussed in Chapter 2, where also some indicators of commonplace current costs per annum are quoted. The purpose of this chapter is to identify criteria for selecting suitable locations, and the actions that will be needed in respect of those locations.

Flexible working, office premises

Hot desking and/or satellite offices are broadly similar in operation to standard office environments, except that they may need:

- more casual parking space (with more movements during the work day) but less all-day parking;
- more personalisation (eg individual lockers) but less personal offices;
- more informal 'conferencing' areas (since they need to function well socially).

The following case study from Digital Sweden (© DEC and reprinted with their permission) features individualised mobile desks to give a sense of ownership to their hot-desking staff.

Digital Sweden — the natural office

Problem

At the Huvbudsta building, members of the DEC site group sat, either singly or with one other member, in rows of glass-fronted, enclosed offices. Communication was poor, except at 10: 00 am and 3: 00 pm, when they used to stop formal work and attend tea breaks for a discussion. They recognised that communications were poor within the group. They were also located away from key contacts in the sales groups in a separate building. In addition, there was in general too much paper within the office, the office design seeming to encourage its retention.

The group moved to the Allen building in January 1992. They had taken a much more entrepreneurial approach to their requirements as dictated by their profit and loss responsibilities as a business, and tackled the fundamental problem of their existing offices.

The solution

A project team of four was responsible for establishing the new office in the Allen building. The design which they presented to the rest of the team was built on four themes. Each of these represented the kind of environment in which the members of the project team felt stimulated and creative. The themes were:

- The archipelago;
- The beach;
- The garden; and
- The golf course.

These themes are depicted in the Natural Office. On the flooring, a central green island is encircled by a sandy beach with blue water at its edges. Over the blue water are ramps, on one side of the office leading to the bridge of the ship, and on the other leading to a quiet room — both raised above normal floor level. On the bridge of the ship are round tables and chairs for informal meetings. This is also where the group meets each morning to have a light breakfast together. The quiet room is glass fronted, carpeted: eight people can gather round a central, angular, irregularly-shaped table. Along one wall, beneath the window, aspirant golfers can get a hole in one on the mini golf course.

A central feature of the Natural Office is a large indoor tree, growing from the garden, with limbs spreading across the ceiling and pieces of fruit hanging from them. Gently press the button on the fruit, and a computer workstation will descend from the ceiling. *En route*, the workstation will be activated and a working light will switch on, both controlled by the BatiBus power system. If there should be a power failure, these can be activated by a battery backup system. The height of the workstation can be adjusted, depending on whether you wish to work standing up or sitting down. If you wish to sit down, there is a variety of chairs to choose from, which allow you to sit in a number of different postures.

Each member of the team has a personal, mobile work desk, with mounted bookcase and drawers. These desks are folded up and stored in a room next to the office, wheeled out when needed, and positioned next to a terminal. Each person also has one metre of shelf space for filing essential items. Things they use often are kept in a bookcase: those needed less often are on the shelves.

Other features of the Natural Office include slatted wooden panelling on the walls, in the same style as many of the houses in the Swedish archipelago. This and the special ceiling help to reduce noise levels. Noise is also reduced by background music, which every two hours gives way to the news. Apart from natural light from the windows, the office lighting is also controlled by the BatiBus system, which adjusts according to the natural light outside.

Cordless CT2 telephones enable DEC site people to walk around the office while holding conversations. The PRESENT system, developed by Digital in conjunction with Presco, also enables them to remain in contact with the switchboard when they are out of the office.

Agile workplaces

The 'Agile Company' is the term used by Texas Instruments to embrace all the various concepts of flexible work. Within this there are a number of concepts of tomorrow's office: Table 5.1 is from John Stanley of Texas Instruments. ✓

Table 5.1 *Concepts of tomorrow's office*

Office concept	Characteristics
Just-in-time (JIT)	Space for work provided on advance notice
Non-territorial	Space designed for short or medium-term teamwork
Caves and commons	Small private places (caves) with shared equipment and meeting areas (commons)
Landing sites	Non-assigned equipped space (telephones, computers)
Free address	Activity centres, space assigned for group-specific tasks
Virtual	Telecommunications make the workplace a state of mind

These concepts embrace the Digital 'Natural Office' described previously and also the IBM 'Touchdown' concept (see text following) which corresponds to the 'landing site'. Clearly the terminology has not settled down yet, and there is scope for new styles of workplace yet to be developed.

Home offices

Where the flexible workers' own homes are to be a work-site, then some consideration has to be paid to the suitability of the proposed ✓

circumstances, and some tact has to be exercised in that consideration. The work-site has to be definable, secure and adequate, both for practical working and in terms of health and safety legislation. It is very important psychologically to flag up very early in a flexible working scheme that people's welfare does not become less important when they are not in the office, but rather that flexible working is entirely geared to maximising welfare and quality of life considerations.

Although the precise nature of the work tasks will determine some aspects of the home based work site, many aspects are common. Key considerations include:

- *Definability* — ideally a separate room, although doubling as a guest bedroom is in practice most common. Modified garden sheds and outhouses are also common — in this case specific actions may be necessary to avoid damage to equipment from condensation overnight.

  One vital consideration is the size of the home: a definable working area is likely to be of 100sq ft (10sq m) minimum, and will more probably be of 150sq ft (15sq m). This is large in relation to the per capita size of dwellings generally. Some typical per capita living space figures in Europe were quoted by the Swedish expert Lonnart Forseback at a symposium in Brussels in 1995 thus:

Denmark	49.9 sq m
Sweden	47.0 sq m
Norway	43.0 sq m
Germany	34.9 sq m
France	31.5 sq m
Finland	30.0 sq m
Italy	29.0 sq m
UK	26.8 sq m
Spain	23.5 sq m

  Clearly, if the per capita average is 26.8sq m, then taking 10 or 15sq m for a home office will not be possible in the average dwelling. Only those households with a genuinely 'spare' room, or with exceptionally generously dimensioned houses, or with outbuildings, are likely to be able to cope easily with accommodating such an office. There is a particular trap here for senior managers of assuming that the domestic arrangements of junior staff (two bedrooms, 60sq m) are the same as their own (five bedrooms, 180sq m) and thus showing a lack of sensitivity to the difficulties arising when junior staff are involved in flexible working implementations.

- *Securability* — this can be achieved by using lockable cupboards and filing cabinets, but a lockable room is less demanding on the discipline of 'closing up' after work. Even where work is non-confidential, the concept of securability enhances the separation of work-life from home-life.
- *Visitability* — inevitably, line managers will sometimes visit the home work-site, and this has to be possible without embarrassment. Female staff in flexible working implementations with male line managers (and vice versa) can create a potential source of embarrassment where the work site is a bedroom: another potential source of embarrassment is untidiness of the home, which can inhibit staff willingness to be visited. It is essential to consider visitability prior to start-up if problems are to be minimised.
- *Legality* — in general, this is not a problem, but it is a very sensitive issue for both flexible working staff and flexible working businesses, so it has to be fully assessed in every individual case. Planning consent will not normally be required if only one room in a house is used for working and if only the residents of the house work there, not other staff. Beyond these bounds, problems will almost certainly arise. Most flexible working businesses would simply choose to avoid having the situation arise, by not entering into arrangements that were not clearly acceptable from a planning point of view. Similarly, most businesses would wish to ensure that their flexible working staff did not incur a Capital Gains Tax (CGT) liability on their home offices: generally, no liability will arise if there is a dual-use of the area concerned, eg if it doubles as emergency guest accommodation by having a sofa-bed in it. In fact, CGT is always likely to be a trivial charge if a working area is only a small part of the home, but as with planning consent it is best simply to avoid the circumstance arising.
- *Safety* — in full accordance with best current practice and with Health and Safety Regulations. Working at home under flexible working terms can involve continuous working periods longer than would be undertaken in an office environment, so

ergonomics become even more important. Legislation that applies in an office generally applies in a home office but even if it did, flexible working staff have a particular need to feel that they enjoy the same levels of support as their office-based colleagues. Key elements that apply here include.

— electric safety checks and certificates;
— ergonomic workstations: include tilt and swivel chairs with adjustable height and footrests; low radiation monitors and wrist supports for keyboards; desks allowing sufficient depth to get the monitor back away from the eyes, and the keyboard well in from the edge of the desk; suitable ambient lighting;
— temperature and, if necessary, humidity control and ventilation (particularly in out-house or garden shed-type locations);
— noise control including screening from the rest of the home if necessary;
— adequate access eg loft ladders into roof-space conversions are not acceptable;
— professional wiring and cabling with supports and cable tidies as appropriate — not miles of trailing leads from distant sockets;
— sufficient working and storage space, room square footage and ceiling height.

Certain areas of guidance and/or training are likely to be needed (and also may well be required under legislation covering visual display unit (VDU) usage):

— formal analysis of workstations and risk assessment;
— health and safety training advice and appropriate breaks (eg ten minutes every hour to be spent away from the screen);
— eye tests on request.

These are all matters that apply equally in the office, so no extra cost arises (and extra costs even in the office are generally very slight): what is needed is only careful consideration.

- *Communicability'* rather obviously, good telephone contact is likely to be required, as also are fax and E-mail links in most cases. Installing an extra line for business use in the home is rarely likely to be a problem, but it is essential to realise that some UK exchanges are still (in 1995) partly analogue, in which case it is necessary to specify that any new line should be a digital line. Unless this is done such features as call waiting, call diversion, feature line etc will not be available (see Chapter 6). Some data-intensive tasks may benefit from ISDN connections, in which case it will be necessary to check on availability: ISDN is generally easily available in towns, but installation costs may be excessive for isolated dwellings in rural areas.

Mobile offices and drop-in centres

Whether these are static or moving, the key features involved are likely to be;

- mobile telephones;
- notebook PCs with modems;
- computer/telephone interaction.

However, some of the aspects of the conventional office will also still apply: insurances will need to be extended from the office location, health and safety aspects will still apply (eg with the use of mobile telephones by drivers), and data security and data protection aspects may require attention. Mobile offices, however, are primarily a matter for technical consideration in (see Chapter 6).

The drop-in centre (or 'Landing Site' to TI or 'Touchdown' to IBM) is a wider concept coming rapidly into general use and offering very obvious benefits. The description of the Bedfont Lake scheme below is by courtesy of IBM and typifies a major development in thinking about flexible work and its impact on office space.

At IBM's Bedfont Lake site, extensive use of hot desking and the fact that a growing number of staff spend some of their time teleworking from home means 1000 staff can operate in a space which IBM in the past considered suitable for only 600 people. However, hot desking is not the ideal solution for all staff, particularly those who are constantly on the road.

Peter Wingrave, IBM's design and construction manager says: 'In the past what used to happen was that if, for example, you were a salesman based in Edinburgh, but had to visit a client in London, you would have to wait until you had flown back to Edinburgh before being able to take any action on behalf of that customer.

'Traditionally, if you had to do something urgently you could come along to our site on the South Bank and talk nicely to a couple of the secretaries to see if they could find you a desk and a PC that was not in use. Very often the owner of the desk would come back half way through or the PC would be locked and you couldn't get into it. It was a very inefficient way of doing things.'

'What we needed,' he continues, 'was somewhere for our employees on the road to touch base.'

Called Touchdown, it serves as a business centre for IBM's salespeople on the road. It offers desk space, hardware and software that is compatible with that used throughout the corporation, photocopying and fax facilities and a phone message retrieval system.

Staff using the area are provided with some privacy through the use of screens, which also have another benefit as they provide an area on which to place information about the facilities on offer and keep staff informed about developments internally.

Mr Wingrave says the space available for a 'drop-in' centre was limited. But IBM selected an area near the staff restaurant where employees had previously gone to smoke and have a coffee. It was important in designing the centre he says, to retain the relaxation element of the space, as well as fitting in the new business technology available.

'Touchdown lets people get together with friends and colleagues over a drink or a sandwich,' comments Mr Wingrave. 'From a corporate point of view, it is very important that people can come in and feel in touch with the organisation and that they are a valued part of it.'

One IBM salesperson says: 'It has changed the way I work. I can drop in between meetings, pick up phone messages, organise all the administrative stuff I have to do for my customers, grab a cup of coffee and visit the loo. But best of all I can catch up with some of my colleagues to chat about work and, more importantly, swap gossip.'

Another adds: 'It can get a bit lonely if you are not constantly with colleagues in an office so Touchdown allows me to meet up with them. It provides a point of contact and it also saves me a lot of valuable time and means that I can process things for my clients much quicker.'

Although the Touchdown space is limited, says Mr Wingrave, it has quite a frenetic vibrancy as those that use it are often in a rush to get to their next appointment.

The area reflects this but also provides a calmer, more relaxing, atmosphere for those who want a quick respite from the rigours of the day. 'Striking the right balance between the fast pace of business and providing a degree of calmness was quite difficult but I think we have achieved that very well,' he states.

Touchdown has also improved the efficiency of IBM employees. The company has not carried out a quantitative study because the main focus of the project was not necessarily to make people more productive. However, surveys carried out among staff indicate that they feel they are using their time more effectively. 'One sales person told me that using Touchdown had saved her up to a week's worth of work,' reports Mr Wingrave. 'If that is true for all the people that use it then that is an awful lot of hours saved.'

The centre has certainly attracted a lot of IBM staff. Since it was launched in 1994 a thousand people a week have used the dozen or so desks available. IBM says that it has proved so successful that it is rolling out the Touchdown concept to its other offices nationwide.

As well as providing its staff with professional services and an area in which to unwind, Touchdown has an added benefit, says the company. The site itself is highly visible from outside the building. Passers-by can glance in and see a fast-moving, modern high-tech environment buzzing with activity, which is just the corporate image that IBM wants to project to the general public.

Locational audit

This is particularly relevant in the case of potential home offices: considerable sensitivity arises in the question of the suitability or otherwise of homes for office use, so an impersonal questionnaire approach in the first instance may help avoid embarrassment later. It is worth noting that much of the information likely to be required is sensitive in the context of the Data Protection Act.

Location audit — questionnaire

Address of the proposed home office location

Flat/house/street ______________________

District ______________________

Town ______________________

County ______________________

Postcode ______________________

Is the property a

- Detached house/bungalow ❑
- Semi-detached house/bungalow ❑
- Terraced house/bungalow ❑
- Maisonette ❑
- Flat ❑
- Other (please specify) ______________

Is it

- Owned ❑
- Rented ❑
- Other (please specify) ____________________

Do you live there

- Alone ❑
- With family/partner ❑
- With friends/sharing ❑

Are there children in the same dwelling?

- 18+, how many? ❑
- 13–18, how many? ❑
- 8–13, how many? ❑
- under 8, how many? ❑

How many rooms are there?

- Bedrooms ❑
- Living rooms ❑
- Bathrooms/toilets ❑

Is the area you could propose to use as an office

- A bedroom ❑
- A living room ❑
- An attic room ❑
- An outhouse or garage ❑
- Other (please specify) ____________________

Is the area subject to heating by

- Gas ❑
- Electricity ❑
- Oil ❑
- Solid fuel ❑
- None ❑
- Other (please specify) ____________________

Is there parking

In a private drive or area	❑
In a shared drive or area	❑
In the street but unrestricted	❑
In the street but restricted	❑
At a distance	❑

Suitability of rooms

Criteria that apply to offices in formal office buildings should equally apply to offices in homes: a good source for information about office environments is the *How to Deal with Sick Building Syndrome* guide. Among the checklist points in this are the following, all of which have relevance to home offices:

- Keep office clean to reduce dust: wet areas of plant including cooling coils and humidifiers (annually), ventilation systems including grilles and vents (annually), windows and light fittings (monthly/quarterly), and internal surfaces, office carpeting, furnishings and furniture including desks and chairs (daily) and deep cleaning of soft furnishings (annually).
- House photocopiers and other equipment away from people.
- Reduce static electricity by treating carpets with anti-static fluid.
- Keep temperature between 20 and 24 °C. Measure air temperature with an ordinary dry bulb thermometer, close to workstations at working height and away from windows. Consider effects of sunlight and of heat emitted from office equipment.
- Erect blinds/curtains on all windows.
- Keep humidity between 40 and 50 per cent. High humidity encourages the growth of harmful bacteria. Low humidity contributes a dusty atmosphere and to dry eyes, nose, throat and skin.
- Damp down noise with mats, covers and screens. Noise generally has a disruptive effect on a workforce rather than being a cause of sick building syndrome.
- Give control over lighting with desk lamps and dimmer switches. Where possible, utilise natural light and avoid glare, flicker and

noise. Offices should be decorated in light, matt colours to add light but cut glare.

- Lay out VDUs to improve views and reduce glare. Supply appropriate lighting.

Using location fully

In addition to the physical suitability of the location, some questions need to be answered which may more easily be handled in face-to-face interviews, concerned with:

- Accepting and welcoming regular visits by a supervisor in the home.
- Accepting occasional visits by equipment maintenance and repair staff in the home.

Other questions, such as that of partner's support or otherwise, child-minding arrangements and so on, fall more naturally into the context of Chapter 4.

Contracts

In Chapter 2 we identified several cost headings where compensation payments would need to be made: in Chapter 4, several areas (status, promotion etc) where arrangements were needed to ensure that flexible workers felt that no detriment would arise to them; and in this chapter questions arose about the acceptance of home visits, maintenance of a safe and suitable working environment and so on.

Checklist for terms

✓

The questions modify the standard content of contracts of employment very considerably, and the following checklist may help to trap out any omissions:

- Definition of duties.
- Payment.
- Pensions.
- Private health insurance.

- Company cars.
- Income Tax and National Insurance.
- Planning requirements and Capital Gains Tax.
- Stationery.
- Postage and telephone charges.
- Access to data and facilities.
- Telecommunications services.
- Maintenance and insurance of equipment.
- Non-disclosure agreements.
- Computer passwords.
- Mortgage.
- Health and safety requirements.
- Union membership.
- Employment protection legislation rights.
- Working hours.
- Duration and review of contract.

Payment

The terms of flexible work contracts should resemble those of on-site workers as much as possible. Businesses may need to demonstrate that their approach is not just a 'cheap and nasty' way of exploiting the services of dependent people. Flexible workers should be paid a fair rate for the job to be done. Failure to do so could result in problems, not only with trades unions but potentially with staff and with clients, and could result in the loss of the services of the individuals concerned.

Where there is an existing scheme of payment by results, this can readily be extended into flexible working. However, where a scheme does not exist, payment by results can be expensive to install and maintain. Because of the personal impact of the change on those concerned, they need to be involved in the scheme's design and introduction. Payment by results will only work if an individual teleworker's output can be measured and controlled and even then, the mere prospect of its introduction may itself be so stressful as effectively to rule out the change.

The no change, no worsening agreement

The economics of flexible work are not in any way dependent on under-rewarding staff; in consequence, the easiest route to quick implementation is to agree to as few changes as possible, and thus to be able to vary the original contract by a simple letter thus:

CONTRACT VARIATION FOR TELEWORKING

To: NAME:

GRADE:

JOB TITLE:

In the context of UK Company plc's flexible work strategy, I am now offering you a variation to your employment contract on the following terms and conditions:

From (date) you will be working from home. This arrangement may be terminated at any stage by UK Company plc, or by you.

There will be no change to pay, hours of work, annual leave entitlement, superannuation arrangements or other employment conditions unless detailed below. Details of existing arrangements are given in UK Company plc's Employee Terms and Conditions publication.

UK Company plc will supply you with all necessary equipment that may be reasonably required to enable your duties to be performed from home. All equipment shall at all times remain the property of UK Company plc, shall not be used for private purposes and shall be returned by you when you cease working from home. All equipment supplied by UK Company plc for use at home will be insured by the Company.

UK Company plc will provide a telephone line for business use which will be paid for by the Company.

You should note that you have a responsibility for your own safety in your home and to ensure that at all times you work in a safe condition. You will accordingly be required to comply with all relevant safety guidelines/instructions and to satisfy UK Company plc that you have done so. UK Company plc will meet all reasonable costs arising in such compliance.

Signed ____________________________

PERSONNEL MANAGER

I agree to the flexible working contract on the terms and conditions stated

Signed ____________________________

Dated ____________________________

Effective dismissal and TUPER

The avoidance of gross changes in contract terms also avoids the risk of effective dismissal (the perceived risk of which is one sure way of killing a flexible working scheme at an early stage) and also helps to keep clear of the rather complex beast called TUPER — The Transfer of Undertakings (Protection of Employment) Regulations of 1981. These regulations can apply in situations analogous to effective dismissal, where there is a transfer of an undertaking from one person to another by sale or 'some other disposition'. This can come into play if a whole department is outsourced and its staff then have a high degree of financial autonomy. Its requirements are no great surprise, in that staff have preservation of service rights, and no diminution of contract terms, but entanglement in TUPER entails a risk of a lawyers bonanza that most flexible working businesses would not happily accept. All-in-all, for the average sort of business, minimal change flexible working contracts can make very good sense, rather than muddying the waters with other simultaneous changes.

Chapter 6

Choosing equipment and services for flexible working

Technical considerations in flexible work — Introduction

The totality of technology available to the flexible working business is at first glance frighteningly large and complex: however, it can be split down into a handful of key areas:

- Computer hardware:
  - PCs;
  - notebooks and personal digital assistants (PDAs);
  - operating systems.
- Computer software:
  - applications (including groupware);
  - communications (including remote access and PC fax).
- Innovative services:
  - E-mail;
  - video conferencing, whiteboarding etc;
  - screen sharing;
  - World Wide Web/Internet.
- Networks:
  - Local area networks (LANs);
  - Wide area networks (WANs);
  - Analog telephony (PSTN);
  - Digital telephony (ISDN);
  - Satellite or very small aperture terminals (VSAT);
  - Cellular (GSM);
  - Radio;

— Fax;
— Electronic data interchange (EDI).

Each of these areas is discussed in the sections that follow.

All flexible working businesses will use some of these, but different subsets apply in different circumstances: generally, the generic choice of equipment will be surprisingly obvious, provided that a good overview of what is currently available is undertaken. The key distinguishing feature of flexible work technology is the communications link to an individual member (ie flexible worker) or to a satellite group of flexible workers, which can mean:

- sending disks by post;
- E-mail (via PSTN, ISDN or GSM);
- file transfer (as E-mail but may also need LAN or WAN);
- WAN link (involves network software or groupware);
- LAN link (almost indistinguishable from WAN these days);
- video-conferencing, screen sharing, whiteboarding etc (probably needing ISDN);
- voice telephony and/or voice mail;
- EDI and fax.

Sending floppy disks by post has declined in popularity to being the last ditch, when-all-else-fails, option, but each of the other technologies still has a place in flexible working.

PC hardware and software developments

Development in this field has been notoriously fast: in Chapter 9 under 'Sciomorphs' the pace of development is discussed more widely, but in the context of procurement of equipment for flexible working there are some pointers to keep in mind at all times.

First, now is always the wrong time to buy: there is always something newer, better and faster just around the corner. This is only a problem until you learn to ignore it, because the numerical figures are so startling that it quickly becomes apparent that there is no answer to it other than to ignore it, as the following example shows.

Typical of the way in which power and size increase while price decreases is the size/price track for commonplace hard disks as fitted to desktop PCs (Table 6.1).

Table 6.1 *Size/price for hard disks fitted to PCs*

Year	Most common size	Typical price
1991	40 Mb	£350
1992	40 Mb	£200
1993	120 Mb	£200
1994	250 Mb	£200
1995	500 Mb	£250

Over the five-year period, the cost in £/Mb has decreased to one fifteenth, roughly halving every year. A cautious buyer would always have foreseen that next year's price would be only half of this year's, and so never bought at all, if that simple logic had been followed. Waiting for prices to 'settle down' means never buying at all.

Software writers have largely stolen back these benefits by increasing the size and complexity of their code, although not at quite such a dramatic rate (see Table 6.2).

Table 6.2 *Some examples of exponential growth in software size*

Software	Lines of code
Microsoft Word v1	27,000
Microsoft Word v6	2,000,000
Microsoft Basic 1975	4,000
Microsoft Basic 1995	500,000

Note: These rates exceed tenfold per decade — see Chapter 9 'Sciomorphs'.
Source: Nathan Myhrvold interviewed in *Wired* magazine.[1]

At the same time, users are simply using more software: a typical user of a desktop PC in 1985, for example, might have had a text-based word processor and a spreadsheet or accounts package — and nothing more. By 1995 this had increased to include also a graphics user interface (Windows, for example), desktop publishing, a diary/address book (organiser) package, a slide presentation package like Power Point, communications and Internet software and a mass of utilities and possibly entertainment packages. The number of users also increases continually at a very fast rate: Figure 6.1 illustrates these growth rates.

In these circumstances there is never any point in waiting for new developments: crucially, what is required is to realise that purchases have extremely short write-off periods. Accountants have long since stopped depreciating IT equipment over ten years, but even three years depreciation is a very questionable policy (the resale value of a three-year-old PC is purely nominal) and the crucial people costs elements (training) are current expenditure and not investment at all, whatever the advertising tells you. The good news, however, is that, if your wants and needs are commonplace, fulfilling them will be very cheap because what was 'specialised' equipment very quickly becomes 'standard' equipment, so that more and more 'specialised' hardware functions (modems, video conferencing etc) will migrate into 'standard' hardware. As a result flexible working applications will be limited not by processor or memory restrictions as they have been in the past but rather by bandwidth availability and cost (see under 'Bandwidth and innovative services').

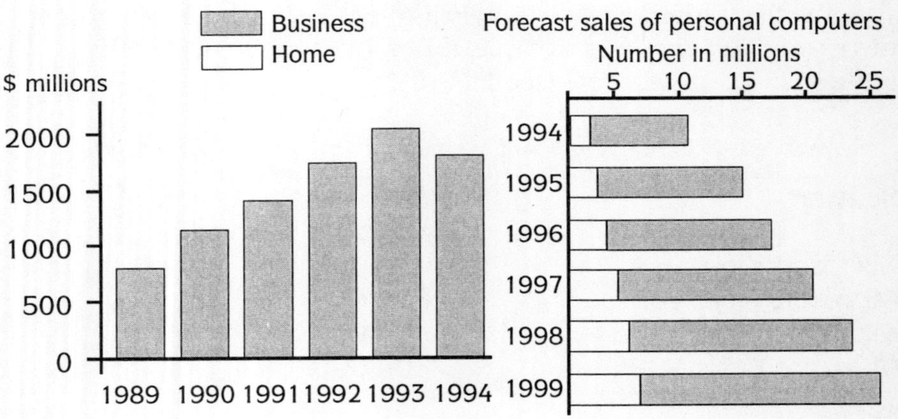

Figure 6.1 *Growth in software (left) and hardware (right) sales in Europe*[2]

Notebooks and PDAs

The origination of these very rapid development rates in equipment performance is microchip technology: Moore's Law says that the number of components on a microchip has doubled every year since 1959 and the end is not yet in sight. One result of this has been size reductions in the physical bulk of components, and hence of both desktop and portable equipment (Figure 6.2).

Clearly size reductions eventually will bring equipment to a desirable minimum size. There is much debate at the moment as to what that size will be, but current sales indicate that the 'notebook PC plus mobile phone' combination is more favoured than PDAs. (A PDA is a personal digital assistant, generally of large hand-held calculator size). Notebook PCs are generally used with Personal Computer Memory Card International Association (PCMCIA) card modems (credit-card sized devices slotted into the notebook PC) for data transmission via GSM mobile phones while on the move. GSM is the European-wide standard (also covering Africa and the Far East) for digital mobile telephony. This is still most frequently used for voice but it was in fact designed for data transmission — which is accordingly relatively cheap by comparison with voice. International 'roaming' makes GSM data transmission particularly attractive for professional and managerial flexible working: the same handset can be used in numerous countries throughout Europe continuously without any reprogramming or other action by the user (except paying for it).

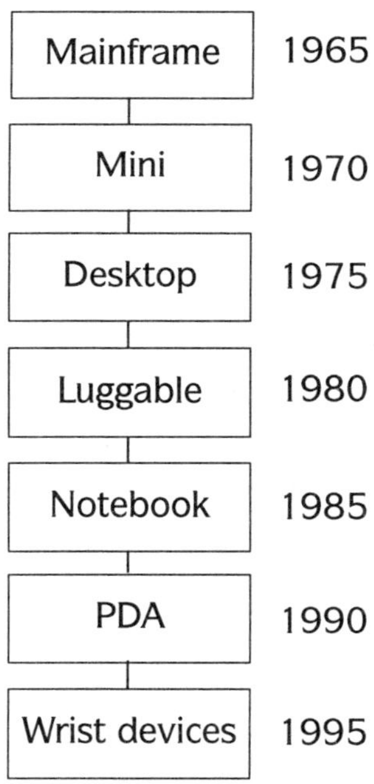

Figure 6.2 *Miniaturising computers in common use*

However, notebooks suffer badly by comparison with desktop PCs in their ergonomic design (and hence, to a degree, in health and safety aspects) by having necessarily small keyboards and screens. They therefore tend to be used either with separate full size keyboards and screens (a very low cost option) when in the 'base' office, or alternatively with 'docking stations' linking to a PC network (docking stations also automatically handle the battery charging).

PCs (taken to include, eg Apple Macintosh and Sun Workstations as well as IBM compatible PCs) are now the normative equipment to such an extent that the only other strategically interesting topics currently under discussion about them relate to operating systems (see below) and to whether or not they should converge with television, rather than about there being any question of their overall desirability or otherwise.

Operating systems

The three key operating systems, UNIX and its variants; and those from Apple and Microsoft, are moving towards more substantial and more stable industrial-strength operating systems, while still maintaining the usability of their current domestic-strength products. This may not be a stable situation: it is easy to imagine that at this very minute a bunch of university students somewhere in the world are testing out a radically new operating system that will eventually make the old dinosaurs extinct: sadly, the only product of this type to appear recently has been a rehash of UNIX that was very good but nonetheless was still yesterday's solution. Until change comes, choices of operating systems are not particularly a significant consideration in flexible working — all have merits, none is yet anywhere near good enough.

Application software

Accessing information

Internet World Wide Web browsers are based on a concept known as 'hypertext', which is a particularly sophisticated use of highlighted key words to link, and to move between, different documents covering similar topics. They represent a move into a new conceptual problem area for information technology, that is the problem of coping with information overload. The size of a commonplace PC hard disk (say 500Mb in 1995) is itself broadly analogous in capacity to a small branch public library: the contents of the largest hard disks in commonplace use in PCs would represent a life-time effort for one person if they were to be read as text files. Being connected to the Internet is like actually living inside the Library of Congress or in the British Library: potentially very interesting and valuable but wholly dependent on good indexing and accessing systems to allow real value to be drawn from all that information. Software development from 1975 to 1995 was largely concerned with efficient processing of 'personal' information, for individuals or for businesses. That phase has been largely worked through, and new products are much more concerned with merging one's own set of data with that of others in a workgroup (Lotus Notes for example), or with coping with the unthinkably great mass of data that represents the world at large (Web Browsers, for example). This new subject has, as yet, hardly been scratched: doubtless the software of 2005 will be quite unrecognisable from that of today. Users of the Internet today will certainly hope so. Another software development still to come is the single comprehensive package of user-friendly communications and network tools for PCs, where a potential market of 25 million users are still making-do with poor quality, dated products, because most of the market leaders started life as UNIX products which were then ported across to IBM compatibles, rather than having been developed as native PC software.

Keyboard and mouse remain as the first choice input methods and will prove hard to shift even as other methods arrive. (It may well be that, as with photocopying, the impetus for change comes from other parts of the world like Japan with more complex alphabets). The widespread use of portable devices (especially notebook PCs) also will be a driver towards non-keyboard input (eg speech), as witness the heavily advertised speech input IBM notebook PC range.

Software programming

New programming methodologies (such as object-orientation) promise cost-reduction in software development but, in general, only deliver rather modest results. In this context, Figure 6.1 reveals that more realistic view of the future for software development: only huge mass markets offer any real prospect in reducing costs for software, and flexible working implementations must therefore stick to mass market products wherever possible to hold prices to sensible levels.

Bandwidth and innovative services

Bandwidth and the super highway

As communication costs drop, so communications demand increases, both for volume (more calls) and also for bandwidth (more information per call). The need for greater bandwidth is generated largely by new innovative services such as video-conferencing and screen-sharing. Flexible working businesses considering such services over the next few years, are likely to concentrate on using Internet-style networks wherever possible. Services such as E-mail, computer conferencing, and Mosaic-style World Wide Web browsers are already in common use either via CompuServe or directly over the Internet. It may be necessary to use specialist value added networks where Internet is not yet functional enough — this applies particularly to real-time applications including video-conferencing, screen sharing, and multimedia databases — but this should always be within a context of migration to Internet-style networks as the Internet itself moves towards becoming a higher-speed information superhighway. Specialist value-added networks make access to new methods easier for novices, but add enormously to costs in the longer term, without offering much compensating advantage.

Although most flexible working businesses still will be almost entirely based in low bandwidth applications (voice, fax, E-mail etc), and so will be able to function perfectly over standard telephone services (PSTN) most of the time, the bandwidth-hungry visual presentation technologies (using ISDN) are the key difference between the 'old' information highway and its newer and more heavily hyped cousin, the information superhighway.

Large corporates in most advanced countries will expect by the end of the century to have broadband links (better than 10Mbit/s) to the information superhighway backbone. However, many workstations in such corporates will still not have broadband links to the company LAN. Small flexible working businesses will expect to have links, either conventional or ISDN-based, of around 128Kbit/s. Very few small businesses had network links to the Internet until 1994, but many now have dial-up links from individual workstations, although those are mostly on PSTN at 144Kbit/s rather than on ISDN. It is still the case in 1995 that it is Sun (or similar) workstation users who consume bandwidth, rather than PC users, but the spread of 64Mb Pentium PCs is changing that situation rapidly.

The situation with ISDN use for flexible working also started to change radically around the end of 1994, with the number of ISDN connections in the UK doubling in the first half of 1995. At the same time, new ISDN 'switches' private business exchanges (PBXs) are coming on to the market which are well suited to the small office and especially to flexible working. These small ISDN switches are described in detail in the section 'ISDN switches for flexible work'.

Video-conferencing

It is unlikely that ISDN will ever become a widely accepted technology for domestic use because many homes may not make the bandwidth jump up from modem speeds, until the next generation of technologies (eg satellite) come into use. In consequence, they may miss out ISDN completely. The specialist equipment for flexible working now being marketed using ISDN standards thus looks rather like a transition phase only: VSAT satellite terminals, digital cellular (GSM) and radio-telephony all seem to offer better long-term prospects. However, as was noted under 'Hardware and software developments', if businesses have an immediate need then they should buy what is available now (and in 1996 that means ISDN) and not wait for tomorrow's dream. Video-conferencing has become a great success in the last few years as its bandwidth requirements have come down to match the basic ISDN capacity. To all intents and purposes, video-conferencing is not available for use other than over ISDN or digital leased lines — it is still not appropriate for use over LANs or the Internet. While there are video-conferencing solutions usable over the Internet, the video quality is poor and the audio quality worse (because audio suffers more than video from the erratic time delays typical of LANs and Internet). Faster Internet links (the superhighway) need to be activated before video-conferencing can be routinely used over the Internet. In the meantime, video-conferencing will tend to be concentrated on 'dedicated' terminals using basic ISDN: adding a video-conferencing set-up to a PC which already has an ISDN link is now relatively cheap (£3000 in 1995) and the price is falling fast as take-up increases.

Screen-sharing

Another technology area which is well-suited to flexible working but where no dominant mass-market solutions have yet emerged is that of screen-sharing. This is where two (or more) users link their PCs so that each can see the others' screens, and also can manipulate them. Like video-conferencing, screen sharing is not well adapted to the Internet because of its real-time nature, but work is going on to solve such problems and new products should come to market over the next few years. Unlike video-conferencing, screen-sharing involves virtually no extra cost in hardware terms. A complementary application that will be important to flexible working businesses is access to multimedia servers (audio and video). This is far less developed than the areas of video-conferencing and screen sharing, far more demanding of real-time performance over networks, and more demanding also of very large hard disk storage on large servers. As a result it is far further from being available over the average level of Internet connection. However ISDN users increasingly have interesting options available using World Wide Web on the Internet (see the next section 'The Internet').

The Internet

Internet is the network of networks, originally set up by the US Defence Department, which now connects most university, many corporate and millions of individual personal and small business computers around the world. It is seen by many governments and by many other thinkers (for instance, Al Gore and Jacques Delors) as the basis of the emerging information superhighway. This is a contentious question: without doubt, however, the Internet is today's information highway, even if not super and therefore all flexible working businesses will have to come to terms with it. Its existence means that no other new widely accepted public-access network is likely to come into existence from now on. (Of course, many other networks are being developed but they will necessarily be so integrated with the Internet and so compatible with its protocols that to the flexible working business user they will seem like just another part of the Internet.) For all the huge volume of publicity surrounding it, there are nonetheless many things wrong with the Internet but these will not stop its growth, although they may well slow it. Inadequate bandwidth on the backbone networks (especially on transatlantic links); inadequate security; inadequate and overloaded servers; and protocols having to cope with tens of millions of nodes and perhaps billions of users, having been designed for only a few thousand, do represent problems. However, work is under way on solving all of those problems, and technical solutions do indeed exist in many cases. The most intransigent problem is that of overloaded servers — at present there is no usable mechanism for load-balancing so that popular databases can be shared automatically across several servers. Another common problem is that flexible working businesses are putting Internet databases on 'domestic' PCs and then struggling when the PCs cannot cope with the incoming 'industrial' network load. These are, however, problems of success (which will attract good solutions quickly), rather than of failure. In the middle term, some sort of catastrophic overload trauma has to be expected on the Internet, but it is still possible to be sanguine about the chances of a post-Apocalypse Internet proving to be as ubiquitous as letter post once was. The killer application on the Internet is undoubtedly the World Wide Web (WWW) which, for once, is a European, rather than American, development. A good WWW browser will allow users to access not only WWW servers, but also gopher and file transfer protocol (FTP) servers, Usenet News and even telnet hosts (for the desperate or old-fashioned). It will also allow the sending of E-mail and the submission of forms for processing. Where E-Mail and file transfer have been the entry level activities for small businesses embarking on communications, and WWW has been their first up-grade point it will quickly become the case that WWW is the entry point and that flexible working business will see WWW as being the whole Internet. One thing that makes WWW so interesting to business is the ability to incorporate audio and video clips into text, thereby creating a wonderful presentation tool; in general, however, it is cheapness, ease of use and functionality that sell it.

Local area networks

Coming back to the more mundane area of internal communication and of data sharing within flexible working businesses, the standard business network for this has been Ethernet, in one flavour or another, but Ethernet is now ageing somewhat. Many businesses therefore are upgrading their Ethernet networks as the load increases on them. There is a 'stretched Ethernet' of 100Mbit/s which is likely to be popular with some flexible working businesses as it offers, allegedly, a relatively easy upgrade path but, for most, more radical solutions will be needed. There are other high-speed LAN technologies on offer such as the fibre distributed data interface (FDDI) (which has been around for some time, without great interest being generated), but the strategic technology most likely to succeed seems to be asynchronous transfer mode (ATM). Despite many worries that this is just 'the next ISDN' (that is, an idea pushed by national telephone companies and standards bodies, but of arguable relevance to real-world businesses), it is likely that, since most telecommunications operators already deploy it and since it actually handles real-time traffic, ATM will be the next strategic LAN technology. There are some risks attached to that prediction, but given ATM's popularity with national telephone companies and in government and European circles, it does seem the most likely medium-term solution. For the time being, however, Ethernet remains the technology of choice but only until say 1997 or 1998, by which time ATM should have become commonplace and the convergence between PC networks and phone networks should be well established.

Wide area networks and LAN interconnect

During the 1980s, end-user networks (ie those used by people over dial-up lines from home or office) were dominated by the old X25 standard. This has already changed, however, and for the foreseeable future they are likely to be dominated by Internet. X25 services are dying away as they fail to compete in bandwidth or cost terms with Internet providers (most X25 services do not even offer 14,400bit/s dial-up, indeed many do not offer more than 2400bit/s, and they charge on both a per-minute and a per-megabyte basis leading to excessive bills, eg for files made with DTP packages). Most Internet services even now offer at least 14400bit/s access (and in some cases 28,800bit/s or ISDN) and charge a flat rate per month. (In some countries Internet providers are still required to levy a volume charge but that practice is in marked decline). Economics thus favour Internet greatly and hence its 1994 growth rate of 10 per cent per month.

The devices used by the majority of flexible workers to access LANs or WANs are modems, but ISDN adapters are gradually penetrating this market. Pundits have for some time been forecasting V34 (28,800bit/s) as the 'final generation' of modems, and this now looks to be the case, at least as far as major improvements of functionality go. Some developers are pushing to the edge, or even just beyond the edge of the V34 specification, looking at speeds of around 34,000bit/s, but there is no great excitement in the market about such a modest percentage increase in performance. As a result, ISDN is at last taking off, with a ten fold increase in the UK in the two-year period mid-1993 to mid-1995, to about 500,000 connections.

ISDN switches for flexible work

Following on from the increased uptake, ISDN adapters are dropping in price and gaining in functionality, so that they can operate at speeds of 57,600bit/s and have as good data compression (V42bis) as modems do. To use such an adapter, a PC or Macintosh has to be able to drive its serial interface at speeds of up to 115,200bit/s or more, and most low-cost personal computers cannot yet do that — indeed many models out in the field are not usable above 11,200bit/s. The obvious solution is to place the adapter on a card and install it inside the computer, but the variety of bus architectures and the increasing use of laptop machines makes this less simple and less cheap than would be desirable. Other methods involve small upgrade (high-speed UARTS — the user agent chips in a PC that control communication speeds) cards for the serial port, or use the parallel port on PCs. The breakthrough for ISDN is likely to come, however, in a rather anomalous way. New telephone switches (PBX) that allow old analogue telephones to be used on ISDN lines will greatly ease the one-off costs of changing to digital systems: a variety of switches at about the £500 level came on to the market in 1995, of which the Racal DAP 6200 is fairly typical, and those represent a breakthrough for the small flexible working implementation.

Schematically, their use is as in Figure 6.3, in which the combination of analog phone, analog fax and digital data can be seen.

The cost-effectiveness of ISDN compared to the next technology step up (the leased line) is very high: tremendously intensive use is required before leased line becomes cheaper, as Table 6.3 (also from an EC study)[3] shows.

Table 6.3 *Cost-effectiveness of ISDN as LAN interconnect solution: peak-hour traffic*

Country	Local	20km	50km	100km	International
France	1.7	6.9	2.2	2.1	7.9
Germany	12.5	5.3	8.5	3.4	6.7
Italy	8.7	2.3	2.5	2.6	10.8
UK	4.8	8.0	3.8	3.0	3.2

Table 6.5 shows how many hours per day of call connect are required in each country and over each distance category before a 64Kbit/s digital leased circuit becomes cheaper than an ISDN switched connection paid for by the minute. The figure assumes:

- peak-hour call rates;
- international calls to destinations within Europe.

On virtually every route it is more cost-effective to use ISDN if the call connect time is two hours or less per day. On international routes and in Germany ISDN is especially attractive. Call connect times of six hours or more per day are required on these routes to justify a digital leased circuit. Six hours of data traffic at ISDN transfer speeds is an immense quantity of data, such that very few flexible workers' applications would come anywhere near it.

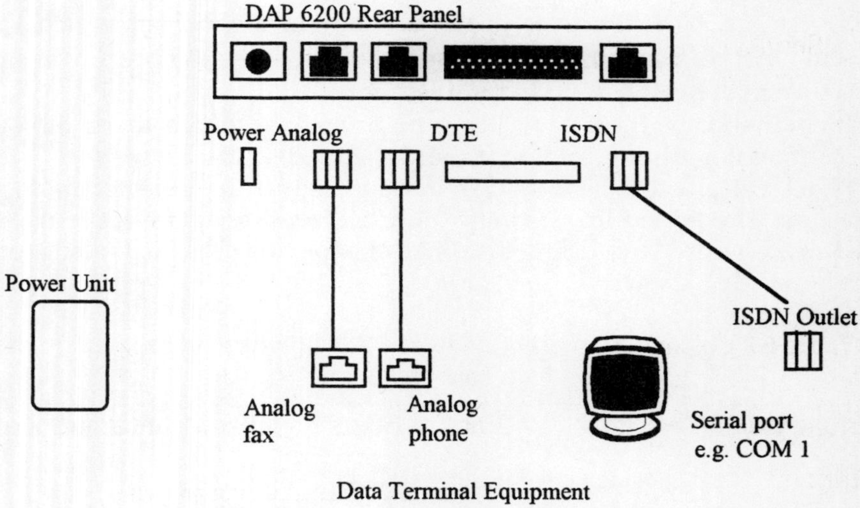

Rear view of the DAP 6200 from Racal DataComm

Figure 6.3 *Analog device interfaces for ISDN*

Multiple subscriber numbering (MSN) (sometimes called just 'directory numbers') allows the use of a continuous run of phone numbers on one site to connect directly to specific devices (phone, fax, data communications etc), so that:

01234 567891 might be a phone;

and 01234 567892 the fax machine;

and 01234 567893 the data line;

and so on. This is a neat and impressive feature which has, to date, had very little uptake outside corporates and local authorities: the advantages in connecting flexible workers over dispersed networks are obvious, however, and the service is very cheap (£20 connection, £10 per quarter in 1995).

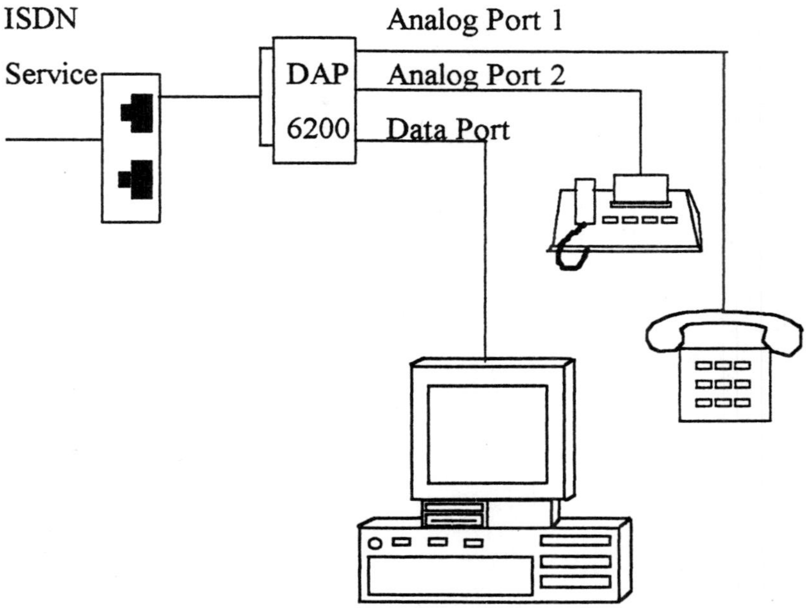

Figure 6.4 *Scenario 2: telephone, fax and PC using MSN*

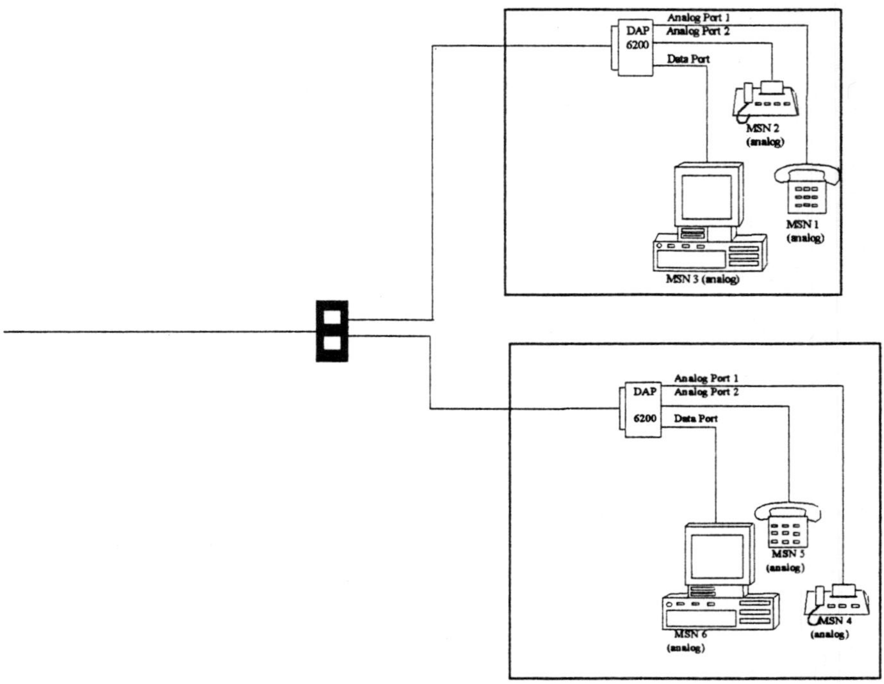

Figure 6.5 *Scenario 3: single ISDN service provided for multiple users*

Table 6.4 *Suitability of individual applications for LAN interconnect via ISDN*

Application	Suitability for ISDN	Demand for application
File transfer	Good	Strong and high growth
E-mail and attachments	Good	Strong and very high growth
EDI	Good	Limited but high growth
Groupware	Good	Very limited but high growth
Terminal evaluation to mainframe	Good	Declining
Video communications	Good	Problems running real-time video on LAN
Transaction processing	Poor — not cost-effective	Very strong and steady growth
Client server	Poor — often not cost-effective	Strong and high growth

Mobile networks — satellite, radio and cellular telephony

Satellite (VSAT) networks are little used in Europe but have advantages for reaching remote areas and for data distribution. At the current level of technology they cannot offer links above 2Mbit/s at affordable tariffs, as compared with their competitors. (The cost of satellite bandwidth is proportional to the bandwidth; on terrestrial circuits the cost is roughly proportional to the square root of the bandwidth, that is, only twice the cost for four times the bandwidth.) Radio networks and cellular telephones, especially GSM telephones, are likely to be the major development area for flexible workers wanting remote access to LANs and WANs (Table 6.5).

Table 6.5 *Broadcast technologies for flexible work*

Technology	Direction	Immediate transfer of data
Pager	1 way	yes
Mobile phone	2 way	yes
Satellite voice	2 way	yes
Mobile data	1 or 2 way	yes
Laptop/fixed modem	1 way	no
Laptop/mobile modem	1 way	no
Palmtops	1 way	yes
PDA/satellite link	1 or 2 way	yes
Band 3 radio	2 way	yes

The breakthrough application here is the PCMCIA card adapter specifically configured to connect notebook PCs to GSM mobile phones: Nokia are one manufacturer offering a turnkey solution to the hardware and software, limking with Mercury to give a fully configured system for data transfer that is not only ideal for mobile flexible workers but is also cost-effective for the occassional home worker or for those with low or occassional data transfer needs. Other manufacturers are following, but some cards work only at 2400bit/s, and these offer no ral advantage in flexible working, where the 9600bit/s of the Nokia version is a minimum standard.

As with digital PSTN phones, GSM offers subscribers a number of 'special services', including:

- Call forwarding: which allows you to have calls diverted to any national or international phone number. This service is useful when the subscriber is not reachable, is busy or when there is no reply.
- Call waiting: if you are already on the phone and someone else is trying to get through, the phone will 'beep' to let you know. You can then put the first person on 'hold' to talk to the escond person if you need to go backwards and forwards between the two calls.
- Call barring: allows you to prevent various categories of outgoing and/or incoming calls (eg premium rate numbers or international calls).

Voice Mailbox is an automated answering service which takes your calls when the mobile is switched off or out of coverage, enabling you to retrieve and play back your calls later. It will also tell you if you have a new message in your mailbox, which you can then play over the phone when roaming. (Cellnet calls this facility Callback, while with Vodafone it is known as Recall.)

Messaging GSM phones can also act as a message terminal. The Short Message Service (SMS) allows messages of up to 160 alphabetic or numeric characters to be received and displayed, even when you are speaking on a call. The message display is ideal as an alternative to paging, asking you to ring a particular number, or passing on a message. It can also tell you when you have voice-mail waiting.

Notebook/GSM data usage had previously been held back by the high level of technical knowledge needed to make the link between the different elements of the system, a difficulty which came from the existence of too many different standards. The whole area of mobile networks has been bedevilled by this standards problem with competition between:

- analog cellular;
- digital cellular (GSM);
- analog cordless;
- digital cordless;
- mobile satellite;
- trunked mobile radio;
- paging;

and so on and on, all with precious little common ground. The EC's Research in Advanced Communications in Europe (RACE) and Advanced Communication Technology and Services (ACTS) programmes address this with the concept of the Universal Mobile Telephone Standard (UMTS) which may, to some extent, be seen as an extension of the successful GSM concept. UMTS products will come to market from 1999 on, at which stage mobile networks can be expected to dominate flexible working in those geographical areas where laying fibre optic cable is prohibitively expensive. Since that is likely to include 90 per cent of the world's land area, UMTS is very much a development to watch. Until then, GSM remains the one key technology with genuine transnational portability.

Fax, EDI and PSTN

It is tempting to write off technologies as old hat as soon as apparently superior new ideas come along, but both fax (hopelessly outdated) and EDI (rather long-in-the-tooth) are thriving mightily and look to have bright futures still. Fax usage finally overtook postal services (by number of messages) in the USA in 1993, and E-mail will do the same in 1995: fax software in PCs is a good gap-bridging technology which can be expected to continue for many years yet. Similarly, EDI, with its rigidly structured, internationally agreed message formats now looks a bit of a dinosaur, when compared with the flexibility of E-mail or the Internet. However, many circumstances in business do actually need very rigid structuring (daily re-ordering by retail stores, for instance) and will go on using EDI indefinitely, albeit that message formats will become wider and more versatile. For most flexible working businesses, 'hard' EDI is a dead letter unless they have major clients who insist on its use.

Virtual private networks

Finally, the one vital technology that it is all too easy to ignore is the plain old fashioned telephone, still the number one tool today and likely to remain so for many years. Flexible working tends to disperse staff away from the central locations that were previously served by sophisticated PBXs (private business exchanges); achieving the same sophistication of switching with flexible working and dispersed staff however can be achieved largely through VPN technology. The main product available in the UK is BT's Feature Line, which gives much the same list of special services that appear above under the GSM section 'Mobile networks — satellite, radio and cellular telephony'.

Additional functions available with Feature Line include Three Way Call which allows three people to speak simultaneously, without having to install conference equipment, and Local Link, enabling a business group to link up to five offices, with free phone calls between offices.

These functions are achieved by software wizardry at the exchanges, so there is no additional equipment requirement for the flexible working business (and also cost levels are accordingly low).

Other features and options available with Feature Line include Direct Inward Dialling and Call Barring. With Direct Inward Dialling, business advertising in *Yellow Pages*, for example, can have all calls to that number quickly transferred to the appropriate extension. The caller can then be given the direct inward dialled number, freeing up the main enquiry number for new business.

Call Barring gives customers more control over their phone network: businesses which deal on a national basis, like taxi firms or restaurants, can make all the calls they need but can ensure that staff do not make expensive unauthorised calls. Using Call Offer, a secretary can filter calls, ensuring busy executives only answer their most important ones. The Transfer to Busy function is ideal in a busy team, allowing the person who picks up a call for a colleague to put the caller on hold and still make calls themselves. The Hunt Group option, includes Cyclical Hunting, which ensures calls are spread evenly around the team.

These facilities are all commonplace in large centralised offices: VPN technology makes them available across a dispersed organisation, combining the benefits of a sophisticated PBX with those of 'virtual leased lines' to give a very powerful flexible working tool.

Making the buying decisions

Whatever the technology being bought, some broad principles apply:

Saloon or sports model?

Unless you have very good reason and the specialist knowledge to back that reason, buy a family saloon: in other words, buy the commonplace, boring, middle-of-the-road stuff that is well understood and well supported everywhere. Similarly, do not buy 'Rolls Royce' unless you have money to burn: you are most unlikely to be able to justify buying the best — what you actually want is the most appropriate, and that is always likely to be rather commonplace.

Standards and architecture

Commonplace means mainstream standards and mainstream architecture, particularly:

- Euro-ISDN for data telephony;
- GSM for mobile telephony;
- Power PC or Intel for PCs;
- MsDOS, System 7, Windows or UNIX for operating systems;
- Microsoft or Lotus for standard software.

Note: The use of the proprietary registered names of Microsoft, Apple, IBM and Lotus are acknowledged here.

Service

Any mission critical item must be provided with full service availability included — and the increasingly rare and expensive breed of people called service engineers do very much like to deal with commonplace things that they see every day, and perform much less effectively with the rare and exotic.

Price

The news-stands are full of magazines that give an excellent guide to the prices of commonplace PC hardware and software, but telephony equipment (other than mobiles) is a rather dodgy, 'Arthur Daley-esque' field where the big telephone companies will try to charge to the limit of your credulity. One good rule is never ever to buy on lease from a telephone company — many businesses are still saddled with hopelessly outdated PBXs from the 1980s because they cannot get out of the lease. Faced with the choice between leasing the ideal choice of equipment from a telephone company, or buying less-than-ideal outright from an equipment supplier, then still do not lease — next year buying new and better may well cost less than one year's rental this year.

Chapter 7

Training for flexible working

Training and encouraging — who needs training?

It is probably not possible, and certainly not wise, to consider introducing flexible working into a business without either previously or simultaneously accepting that the business has to move into a routine of lifetime training. Most professionals (accountants, doctors, nurses, teachers and so on) have to undergo some training activity every year if they are to continue working: this is the new world of training, in which training is a continuing process, occupying typically two full weeks of each year in keeping staff up to speed with developments in their own specific field of activity.

Training for flexible working therefore needs to be seen in the context of an organisational structure in which training is a normal and commonplace activity, not a one-off event associated with some upheaval. (The idea of re-training after redundancy, for instance, identifies the problem rather than solving it: to what extent did the lack of training create the redundancy situation?) Given the existence of an environment where training is normal, then tailoring it correctly becomes a relatively simple task. If the idea of a continuing training environment does not exist, then flexible working may be contraindicated.

Many fears about flexible working are the product of lack of familiarity; the idea that staff working at a distance will suddenly become irresponsible and sit around doing nothing, for instance. However, if staff are inadequately trained and simply do not know what to do, then working at a distance could easily magnify that existing problem into a disaster.

Because flexible working involves changes in business philosophy, not just changes in working methodology, it is likely to create training needs evenly through the whole business, ie for

- directors and principals;
- managers;
- supervisors and group leaders;
- flexible workers.

Within these groups, it is important to understand the degree of motivation present and to encourage and stimulate motivation where necessary — to pull flexible working through the organisation, not to push the organisation into flexible working. Historically, the most likely blockage area has been line management: directors and principals will be committed to the efficiency gains, flexible workers will see practical and personal development gains, and group leaders will see enhanced status and better working conditions. Managers, however, may see merely a threat to their autonomy: if their training and motivation is omitted or inadequate, information will not flow as it should and schemes will be endangered: the biggest threat to any flexible working scheme is surly line-management.

Training and encouraging — what competences are needed?

In a study carried out by the Flexible Work Company for the National Council of Educational Technology,[1] the various competences needed were grouped under the acronym TOP:

- **T**ask competences.
- **O**perational competences.
- **P**ersonal competences.

These categories often overlap considerably, so that training in one area may well impact on each of the others, but the TOP split is at the least a good basis for analysis. Different individuals in the organisation will need different weights of emphasis on these areas (Table 7.1).

Task-based competences

At first glance the introduction of flexible working has little effect on the need for task skills — authors still write, designers still draw and so on. However, in practice the introduction of flexible working tends to intensify existing pressures towards the ever-increasing use of technology in implementing those skills, so that authors are pushed further into sophisticated word processing and even DTP skills; designers into the direct manipulation of digitised images; and so on. This is no more than a change of emphasis, but it does mean that existing training qualifications (eg National Vocational Qualifications (NVQs)) have to be looked at with a rather jaundiced eye to see if they have been updated adequately to modern conditions. It was still the case in 1994 that office skills NVQs, for instance, referred to the use of telex, which led to some interesting scenes as companies tried desperately to locate a telex set-up that was still in use. By and large, however, the existing NVQ framework is likely to remain adequate for task-based competences.

Table 7.1 *Competence levels and training required*

	Task	Operational	Personal
Directors and principals	Light	Heavy	Medium
Managers	Medium	Heavy	Medium
Supervisors and group leaders	Medium	Medium	Heavy
Flexible workers	Heavy	Light	Medium

Operational competences

This is the extension beyond task skills, to those skills necessitated specifically by flexible working: it can be hard to draw a precise line between this and the extended task skills identified above, particularly where organisations already make heavy use of modern communications equipment. It is generally the case that operational changes are associated with the progressive introduction of new technologies, so that training may be needed in the use of:

- personal computers generally;
- PC communications, including the use of data modems and fax modems;
- dedicated fax machines;
- sophisticated telephone systems including answerphones, feature phones, ISDN etc;
- voice mail systems;
- E-mail systems and the Internet;
- video-conferencing, whiteboarding etc;
- group working software.

All organisations will possess some or all of these technologies already: flexible working imposes a step-wise, rather than gradual, progression up the technology scale, however, so there will always be new requirements for:

- at the least, familiarisation demonstration;
- generally, some specific user training, possibly from the supplier;
- occasionally, in-depth training, which will almost always be 'bought-in' from specialist training suppliers, usually at some expense.

Personal competences

This is the real nitty-gritty for flexible working: one key area is concerned with personal development and would include:

- presentation and communication;
- avoidance of the atrophy of professional skills;
- coping with isolation from office politics;
- self motivation.

The other key area of training need is concerned with the effective change in organisational status of the flexible worker from corporate employee to autonomous business unit, and has many parallels with the generality of small business start-up training:

- time management;
- financial planning and budgeting;
- internal accounting;
- reporting and invoicing.

Traditionally, it has been the case that these general business skills have been acquired by a process of osmosis as individuals have moved through career development paths, but the introduction of flexible working makes a sudden step-wise progression necessary (just as it does with operational skills) and the suddenness of that step may necessitate a move from implicit to explicit training.

Personal competences — group competences

A further sub-grouping of the personal competences required relates to working in groups: group working and flexible working are increasingly synonymous terms. Developing teams of flexible workers necessitates considerations of psychological profiling and of team dynamics, questions which are important in choosing people for flexible work (see Chapter 4). Particularly where multidisciplinary teams are concerned there will be a matching training requirement for team working. This training can only be fulfilled satisfactorily in the working environment and in teams. Training in personal competences will thus normally involve bringing in teams of specialist human resource trainers to work on-site in the business.

One of the most sensitive and crucial areas of flexible working training specifically involves managers and group leaders: new leadership styles have to be inculcated which are based on auditing and monitoring, rather than on supervision. Such leadership styles are inherently less control-oriented and thus allow flexible working staff greater autonomy. Training must not only provide the tools for this, but also induce a high degree of commitment to such leadership patterns. A further key 'group competency' question is quality management — see 'Quality Management Issues' following.

Hardware-user training

Dealing first with the easiest of the training needs, the subject of training related to the use of hardware has traditionally been the province of suppliers and in-house trainers. There are, of course, continual rapid changes in the pattern of hardware in use, as Figure 7.1 shows.

It is interesting to see how both fax and modem use increased very suddenly: this is a common phenomenon for communications hardware. Small businesses will delay buying because there is 'no one at the other end', ie their business partners do not yet have the item. Once they start to buy, the growth is explosive over a very short period of time. For a further example of this phenomenon, in 1995 it is the case that video-conferencing is relatively cheap (about £3000 per unit) but its take-up being much inhibited by the 'no one at the other end' syndrome. Sometime in 1996 or 1997 a critical mass of users will be reached such that the explosive growth phase suddenly will be reached.

During such explosive growth phases, small business journals and news-stand magazines will be full of articles about the hot item of the day (as they were in 1995 about Internet) and this creates a self-training mode which is both important and (arguably) often sufficient in this context.

Until the explosive growth phase is reached, however, most training in the use of hardware will necessarily come either from suppliers as part of the sales package, or from third-party training specialists.

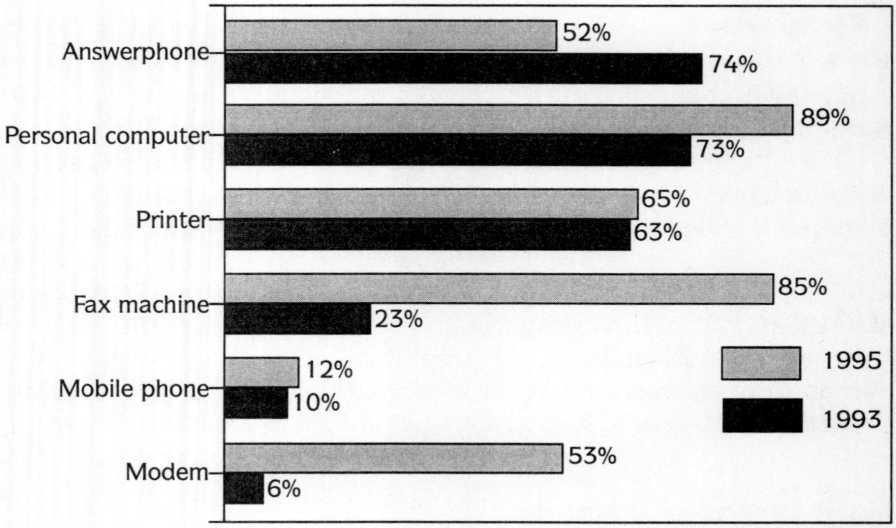

Note: Not exactly comparable figures from two different surveys.[2,3]

Figure 7.1 *Equipment for teleworkers in 1993/1995*

Software-user training

This differs very markedly from hardware user training: there will be the same intensive training requirement at the time of first implementation, handled in the same way as hardware user training, but subsequently there will normally be a continuing requirement for refresher training to

- maintain infrequently used functions;
- accommodate upgrades;
- introduce new tasks;
- introduce improved routes to old tasks.

Effectively, such training has to be designed in-house because it will be very specific to the business needs. Typically, one week every six months may be dedicated to such top-ups.

Software for time management

Time management is a key area in flexible working; not just the ability to 'self-start' and to use time effectively, but also the converse skill of 'self-stopping' and turning off when work is finished. Many flexible workers, particularly when working at home, fail to make the distinction between work time and leisure time — usually to their disadvantage rather than that of the employer. In the longer term, however, over-working can damage the employer as well.

Software tools for time management are an ideal aid to introducing time discipline: on-line time can be monitored and logged, and off-duty periods and vacations can be highlighted clearly and protected.

Software for communications

Just as software can be used to introduce the topic of time management skills, so it can also be used to introduce the topic of communications skills. In the course of training in the communications techniques dictated by the flexible work tasks, concepts such as 'social cues'; dealing with 'troubles'; and 'communication acts' can be introduced, and thus routes to overcoming the impersonality of telecommunications and hence to overcoming the potential isolation problems of flexible working can be identified.

Technology-based training

Flexible working implementations lend themselves particularly well to the use of computer-based training (CBT) or technology-based training (TBT), which can offer considerable advantages:

- Learning at the student's own speed. Flexible working staff are all individuals with different levels of practical and academic experience, and learn different things at different speeds. Peer-group pressure in a classroom situation can result in trainees skimping on topics they find more difficult, in an attempt to 'keep up'.
- Learning when and where the student wants to. The demands of business mean that it is difficult to set aside days (or weeks) to attend courses which often have to be booked months in advance. If a booked trainee cannot attend due to some crisis, either the course fee may be lost (in whole or part) or a substitute

may be sent 'to use up the place'. Neither of these alternatives is good for trainees, their employing organisations, or the organisation running the course.

- Avoiding the cost and inconvenience of travelling, hotels etc.
- Revising and referring as the student needs to. If flexible working staff go away on a lecturer-led course they probably return with just a set of photocopies of the overhead projector foils used, or maybe with a 'work-book' of examples. Distance learning courses are available complete for revision and reference at any time later.

Desktop training, delivered by multimedia computers, offers these advantages as well because it is a form of distance learning. In the past, distance learning (for instance by 'correspondence courses') had some problems:

- It was difficult and/or expensive for traditional distance-learning methods to assess and guide trainees. For example, the Open University requires students to submit assignments for review by tutors. The vast majority of these assignments are submitted by post, and returned by post, giving feedback delayed by weeks. A TBT course, however, can monitor progress continuously, prompting, assessing and guiding the trainee, giving instant feedback and recording assessment results for later review. For high-tech topics, a drawback of traditional distance learning is the near impossibility of providing practical exercise.
- Traditional distance learning based on paperwork is not easily updated. For a fast-moving technology like telecommunications, this is a serious drawback. TBT, on the other hand, can be designed for easy updating ' diskettes can be rewritten easily with revised material, and CD-ROM based courses can include 'hooks' to allow new material to be added from diskettes — or from a server on a LAN.
- Some distance learning courses include audio and video tape sections. These add welcome variety and extend the capability of the course to present material — for example, language teaching is unthinkable without the trainee being able to hear spoken dialogue. It is not easy, though, to ensure that the trainee is playing the right tape at the right time. Also, there is, perhaps, a more subtle element: audio and video tapes are normally used to entertain, not to instruct; therefore, it may be that trainees become passive when viewing or listening to a tape. Modern

TBT with integrated video clips and built in audio, presented on a computer screen, can overcome these difficulties.

- Another area in which TBT can excel is in testing and recording of student activities. Of course, it is not possible to prevent a determined attempt at cheating, but PTTs SyncNet[4], for example, records test results, and the time spent on various activities and stages reached by each trainee, on his/her own trainee diskette. On completion of the course, the trainee can get a transcript in the form of a printed Certificate of Achievement.

Topics for training modules

The NCET publication, *Training for Teleworking*[1,] describes 14 training 'units' covering:

- What is teleworking?
- Self-management.
- Project/team working.
- Communication skills.
- Technology.
- Legal/regulatory framework.
- Business skills.
- Managing teleworking schemes.
- Team building.
- Project management.
- Teleworking supervision.
- Training and updating.

These units represent a good starting-point for the design of specific training modules tailored to the needs of the individual business, and covering both the initial implementation and the ongoing management of flexible working schemes. At the pre-pilot stage, the requirement for implicating the staff as early as possible can also be met by introducing a 'training' document which describes the whole topic in outline, in which what is most needed is to get across the 'flavour' of flexible working, so that people can assess for themselves how they might perform. Service and equipment suppliers produce much literature of this type (see also Chapter 8 for details). In one such set of documentation, Francis Kinsman (in Mercury's

The Flexible Working Portfolio[5]) sets out ten key points for flexible workers: these make a good basis for giving people the feel of how it might work for them to work at home (assuming that it is home that is to be their work site).

1. There are no office conventions or timings any more. Work can be fitted around your own lifestyle. If you have domestic demands, answer both by organising your time. Forget 'either/or'. An efficient 'both/and' is possible.
2. Are you a lark or an owl? Working from home means you can adapt to the rhythm that suits you best, by starting and ending early or late. At low energy times, tackle something short and easy and feel achievement at having done it.
3. Keep a personal time log of your working day in the office and at home, and then compare the two. See how long you spend on social niceties in the former, and on coffee, snacks and domestic issues in the latter. Monitor and analyse your time usage at least weekly. What areas of weakness should you be addressing?
4. Don't be too hard on yourself — you won't change overnight. Take five-minute breaks, maybe as often as half-hourly to begin with. Working at home is more demanding until you get used to it; go on too long and you risk quality slippage. Don't go at it like a bull at a gate, and take time to think.
5. First thing before starting work, think about making a break between the domestic and the working day. Enjoy the garden for five minutes, or walk to buy a newspaper. Then instead of the ritual office greetings at reception, mail-opening and coffee chat, evolve your own equivalent home rituals — such as the contemplation time at start up, the twice-daily call to your secretary or a colleague, the times you are definitely available for outside calls, making lists (this doesn't suit everyone) and specific goal schedules, which break up the day's activities.
6. Family, friends and neighbours may get the wrong signals. Nothing is more maddening than the assumption that 'being at home' somehow means 'not being at work'.

React to emergencies, but ensure that you are not automatically available on demand for casual domestic or social reasons. As far as family is concerned, it is best to draw up an agreed contract (written down and signed makes it a solemn covenant with children). This sets out the timing of your routine and emphasises the fact that except in case of fire or Martian invasion, you are not to be disturbed unless you invite communication.

7. Leave the answering machine (you must have one) switched on while you are working. If it allows you to hear the incoming message, you can screen it and decide whether you want to pick up the call. If it doesn't, you can always play it back immediately afterwards and then decide. Meanwhile, when telephoning out, prepare each planned call, and make notes in advance.
8. Spend 10–15 minutes last thing considering tomorrow's key challenges, and establish priorities for the beginning of the day. Make sure you will have the right documents with you if you are planning to work at home tomorrow after working at the office today (and vice versa). Plan deadlines for the most crucial tasks, working backwards — but always allow a margin for the unexpected and be alert for time-bombs. Compulsive list-makers can miss out on this.
9. What do you do with the three-quarters of an hour plus each day that you are saving by not commuting? Does it belong to you, the organisation, or both? Think about it, agree on it, then work or relax, accordingly.
10. Finally, encourage yourself with the idea that working from home, you will be a whole lot better at managing your time in any capacity. Think about that too, in terms of your career and life purpose.

Source: *The Flexible Working Portfolio.*[5]

Quality management issues

Many businesses introducing flexible working will already have quality systems in place: this makes flexible working easier in that much prior analysis of processes will necessarily have been done, and the relatively small changes needed in existing quality systems to incorporate flexible working are easily made. Where no formal quality management system exists, it makes sense to consider implementing one prior to the flexible working implementation, not least because of the extent to which the analysis requirements overlap. A number of quality management 'products' exist in the flexible working arena which may be applicable particularly where outsourcing or subcontracting are inherent in a flexible working scheme. Most are based on BS5750/IS900*x* series standards. What follows is extracted from the National Association of Telework's quality management for teleworking (QMT) standard[6] with their permission: it is very much geared around small (<20) autonomous groups, which is the flexible working norm arrangement.

QUALITY MANAGEMENT for TELEWORKING (QMT)

In the document that follows, specification clauses (ordinary type) are preceded by explanatory notes in italics.

0 Introduction and Scope

Note 1: The QMT Specification

Reading through the QMT specification, it is tempting to observe that it is no more than common sense, albeit expressed in a very formal, even pedantic fashion. This is a correct perception; there is nothing in QMT, or in any other well thought out quality management scheme, which should offend against common sense. The same is true of all formal business and management studies; you could work it out for yourself quite easily. Given time, that is. Given enormous amounts of time; and even then you would have a scheme which, though doubtless well tailored to your personality and your business, had no direct interchangeability with other schemes and had no external stamp of approval. QMT is not only about the way your business is run, it is also about the way it is seen to be run and the way it interfaces with other businesses, be they clients or suppliers. It is just common sense, but it is common sense that is formalised, standardised, and conforming with external standards.

0.1 QMT is the approved guideline of the National Association of Teleworkers for the application of a quality system to the teleworking environment. The structure and contents of this approved guide are designed to interface with the minimum requirements of ISO9001, EN29001 and BS5750 Part 1 or any derivative thereof where possible.

0.2 QMT forms the basis of the National Association of Teleworkers' Quality Management for Teleworking Certification Scheme.

0.3 QMT is applicable in contractual situations where specified requirements, consistency of operations and capability require demonstration, accountability and visibility. For the purposes of this guide a contract can exist in both an employer/employee or purchaser/supplier situation.

0.4 QMT recognises that there are particular characteristics of teleworking that require special interpretation for a quality system to be effective.

0.5 QMT assumes that any standards to be met between the contractual parties have been specified and agreed. QMT further assumes that the contract (and the parties to the contract) is fiscally sound and will have no bearing upon the contract performance.

Note 2: Introduction and Scope

It is worth noting (0.3) that QMT necessitates a 'contract': contract in the sense could be a formal contract, a written purchase order, or a contract by letter, but some contract must exist and be evidenced. If the work was ordered verbally, then a formal note of it must be kept and a written acknowledgement made. ***Getting a routine of formal acknowledgement of all orders and variations is, therefore, an essential prerequisite for QMT.***

In section 0.5 it should be noted that QMT does not set standards. These are negotiated between the contracting parties. QMT, as with other quality management systems, is concerned with meeting the stated and implied needs consistently. Fiscal soundness (eg is it realistic that the work should be done at the price quoted?) is not strictly part of QMT, but without it, contracts become nonsensical, and that can undermine any system of quality assurance. ***Implementing QMT clearly implies not taking on work at suicidal prices.***

Definitions

Purchaser	—	is the contractor or employer.
Teleworker (supplier)	—	is the provider of the service.
Teleworking	—	is undertaking contractual obligations at a remote location utilising telecommunication techniques to simulate close proximity.

Note 3

In some contracts, both parties buy and both parties sell to one another. It is essential in operating QMT to know clearly who is the buyer (purchaser) and who the seller (supplier).

QMT requirements

Note 5

This now gets down to the nitty-gritty. Some of the requirements will need further explanation and example during the 'system building' stage, but some can be, at least in part, built in to your day-to-day operation immediately.

2.1 The teleworker will set out in the form of a mission statement, policy statement or code of conduct his/her objectives and commitment to quality.

Note 6

There is a commonplace standard format for this in respect of QMT, but you may wish to consider the general question of a mission statement for your organisation.

2.2 The teleworker will set out in an appropriate form the responsibility, authority and relationships of all persons or legal entities engaged in the teleworking contract. Where it is considered appropriate by the purchaser, this information shall be directly interfaced with the purchaser's organisational details.

Note 7

This is not just a question of knowing who does what: it has to be 'set-out', ie in writing, and everybody concerned has to be at least informally aware (and preferably in agreement) about this. Remember that QMT is a document based management system requiring all key aspects to be written down.

2.3 The teleworker shall establish and maintain procedures so as to ensure that equipment specifications, anti-virus software and software capabilities have the capability to meet contractual requirements.

2.4 The teleworker shall appoint a person, to be known as the 'quality manager' who will have sole responsibility for ensuring that the requirements of QMT are properly implemented and maintained. Where a teleworking contract is between an employer/employee then the purchaser will be required to make such an appointment and the teleworker will provide reasonable access to the quality manager in order that the quality manager can properly fulfil his responsibilities under the quality system.

Note: In the case of a sole teleworker either the teleworker or an approved quality consultant may be the quality manager.

2.5 The teleworker shall review and record periodically the ability of the Quality System to remain suitable and effective in sustaining the current and future contractual obligations of the teleworker (see 0.3).

Note: QMT recognises that in smaller organisations or sole proprietorships, the objectivity of adhering to this section may present difficulties; therefore the adoption of clear and structured procedures is needed in order to demonstrate compliance. Integration with formal business plans created for, *inter alia*, fiscal, marketing or product development reasons is generally recommended.

2.6 The teleworker shall establish and maintain in a documented form all the QMT requirements:

a. A quality management manual detailing the policy and organisational objectives of the QMT requirements.

b. A supplementary manual or series of supplementary manuals detailing the operational details of the QMT requirements.

Note: QMT accepts that where the teleworker is operating under a contract of employment this subsection may be surrendered to the requirements of the purchaser in so far as it is integrated with an approved quality management system.

Note 8

Producing manuals is much easier with help and examples, so most organisations will leave this until the system building stage. However, quality manuals have a 'totemic' place in marketing mythology: start one now, put these documents in it with your notes, draft procedures and the like in them, and then you have 'started building a quality manual'. One day, that might just be enough to tip the balance your way in winning an order, or moving up through your company.

2.7 The teleworker shall establish and maintain procedures to regularly review ongoing and future contracts so as to ensure that sufficient resources can be brought to bear to fulfil obligations as they fall due. Such contract reviews will have regard to any material changes in the law relating to the security of data and material changes in the technologies associated with the teleworking contract in so far as they materially affect meeting the contractual obligations.

Note 9

You have always done this, of course, even if only instinctively. However, under QMT you must:

a. Keep a record of such reviews.

b. Not enter into an undertaking that you cannot reasonably expect to resource.

2.8 The teleworker shall establish and maintain procedures so as to ensure that the design criteria of the purchaser where appropriate to meeting the contractual obligations are undertaken by the teleworker at all times. Where the teleworker is required to undertake to design under the requirements of the purchaser, or the purchaser requires the teleworker to demonstrate design control, then matters concerning design input, design output and design verification and design changes shall be expressed in the form of a quality plan and annexed to the teleworking contract.

Note 10

The concept of 'design' here is very broad indeed. Where you undertake to carry out a whole project by meeting its overall objectives (rather than simply carrying out defined tasks with a project) you will be involved in design. Deciding how to go about the project and meet those objectives is 'design', however far removed it is from drawing and aesthetics, and it has to be formally approved and recorded.

2.9 It is a fundamental requirement of QMT that all aspects of the quality system are documented and recorded. QMT is a document based quality system: documents can either be in the traditional form or any other acceptable media. The teleworker shall establish and maintain procedures to control all material documentation and data issued and used to maintain the quality system and that documentation and data used in the performance of the contractual obligations.

Note 11

You will have realised by now that QMT generates paperwork. Both the documentation related to the work and the documentation relating to QMT have to be tightly controlled. In particular, you need to:

a. find a current document, now, quickly; and

b. in say three years time, find a specific document in use today and be absolutely sure that you have the correct version and who else had it.

This is one of the most demanding aspects of QMT, and one of the furthest removed from most organisations' habitual practices.

2.10 The teleworker shall establish and maintain procedures so as to ensure that all purchases are in accordance with specified requirements having regard to the contractual obligations. Where the teleworker is operating under a contract of employment, QMT recognises that the supplier may impose specific or generic terms and conditions.

Note: Purchases will include work subcontracted (with prior approval) to other teleworkers or to providers of software, hardware or data.

Note 12

It is very important that purchases of any goods and services in a QMT controlled project are specified and controlled. The use of written purchase orders becomes essential (but a duplicate book is often good enough), and you need to know about your supplier's quality status.

2.11 The teleworker shall establish and maintain procedures for each activity or process upon which contractual obligations are undertaken (see 2.2). QMT recognises that the teleworker may be required to adopt a quality plan of the purchaser. In the event that the teleworker is operating under a contract of employment this section will be appropriated from the supplier's own quality system.

2.12 The teleworker shall establish and maintain procedures in matters of quality control in the following specific areas:

a. Goods inwards.

b. Inspection and testing of work being undertaken under the contract as directed under that contract or as reasonably required.

c. Goods outwards.

d. Version/issue control testing, where appropriate, of all equipment used including hardware and software processes.

e. Incorrect work identified during the process.

f. Rejected work.

Note: The teleworker must establish a clear document based trail in order that the points above can clearly be identified for the purposes of undertaking the appropriate corrective action. QMT recognises that these requirements may be specifically stipulated in the contract and may require adoption of the purchaser's own quality system.

2.13 The teleworker shall establish and maintain processes so as to ensure that the quality manager (who may also be the teleworker) has clearly identifiable and structured records so as to record, at a minimum, the following:

a. Management reviews (see 2.5).

b. Quality control results (see 2.12).

c. Internal audit (see 2.14).

These quality records shall be capable of demonstrating the achievement of quality in meeting contractual obligations.

Note: QMT recognises that these requirements may be contractually specified by the purchaser having regard to the nature and characteristic of the process being undertaken.

2.14 The teleworker shall periodically carry out an internal audit of the quality system so as to determine its effectiveness. The internal audit may deal with one or more parts of the quality system on each action but all parts of the quality system must be subject to an internal audit once every 12 months.

Note: QMT recognises the practical problems which arise in the event of a sole teleworker attempting to undertake an internal audit of a sole proprietor operation. It is accepted that in certain situations requirements 2.5, 2.12 and 2.14 may form a single but comprehensive procedure. In the event that the teleworker is operating under a contract of employment these matters may fall under the authority of the purchaser.

Note 13
This is different from management review (2.7); the QMT system assuredly will need to evolve as your business evolves. Internal audit not only checks that it works, it also prevents stagnation.

2.15 The teleworker shall establish and maintain in an appropriate form that information which is necessary to demonstrate the following:

a. Effective use of telecommunication and teleworking techniques.

b. Competence to undertake the contractual obligation.

c. Identification of training needs.

d. Appropriate education.

Note: Records must be maintained of continuing personal/ professional developments.

2.16 The teleworker shall maintain documentary evidence for the purposes of satisfying the purchaser on matters concerning the teleworker's environment, safety and contingency plans.

2.16.1 The teleworker will maintain drawings, descriptive narrative and, where appropriate, photographic records in order that the purchaser can ascertain in sufficient detail that the working environment of the teleworker is appropriate to the nature of the contract.

2.16.2 The teleworker shall maintain in sufficient detail records describing the health and safety and fire precautions undertaken at the teleworking site and its immediate surroundings. Where the teleworker is operating under a contract of employment, the purchaser will ensure that these requirements are maintained within the stated policies of the purchaser's organisation.

2.16.3 The teleworker will set out, in the form of a recovery plan, documentary evidence of the capabilities of the contract to be fulfilled in the event of disasters arising through the failure of the teleworker's systems, prolonged telecommunication failures or the prolonged incapacitation of the teleworker.

2.17 The teleworker should establish and maintain procedures so as to ensure that:

a. All data used in meeting the contractor's services is secure to generally accepted standards.

b. That when contractually required compatibility with the purchaser's specification for the security of data can be demonstrated.

c. All transmission channels and links established for the purposes of delivering data should be secure to generally accepted standards.

d. Traditional methods of handling, storage, packaging and delivery of products and services are such that there should be no deterioration in the delivery of the product or service to the purchaser.

e. The delivery, together with any associated process or activity, of the product or service in either an on-disk, on-paper or by electronic transfer shall be treated congruently within this specification.

Note: Generally accepted standards concerned with the security of data and its transmission will include, *inter alia*, regular changing of passwords and log-on identifiers and the secrecy of original documentation concerning transmission procedures. For the purposes of satisfying this approved guideline it is recognised that these matters should be mutually agreed as between the teleworker and the purchaser and expressed specifically in the contract.

Chapter 8

Creating a trial implementation

Implementing a flexible work trial

It is vitally important to remember that the question on trial here is 'How best can we make this work?' not 'Will this work?' (If there were still real doubt about flexible working's potential for the business, a trial would be premature.) The first stage of a trial is therefore the prior review of implementation strategy, that is of how to make it all work.

Trials and pilots naturally tend to be tied to pre-prepared budgets, but this itself carries a degree of risk: flexible working is a changing, moving target where advantages accrue from flexibility, so it is important to avoid an excessive rigidity of implementation. Another risk factor to be avoided in trials is excessive investment in today's technology, to the extent that subsequent change to yet newer technologies becomes an embarrassment. Finally, in the context of risks to be avoided, it is important to avoid equating flexible working to only one 'flavour' — teleworking alone say, or touchdown centres alone. In all probability, most businesses eventually will implement several routes to flexible working, not just one.

Strategic review

✓

Reviewing flexible working strategy is very much easier in those businesses where strategic review is commonplace, but even if the business has little in the way of long-term planning the implementation of flexible working still needs strategy. Among the strategic questions to be raised would, for instance, be the expected size of the workforce and its profile from a skills viewpoint; the size, location, and degree of commitment to premises; and/or the possibility of moving client support staff out to work directly with clients.

Unless the answers to these questions are available 'off-the-shelf', which in the real world is rather unlikely, then finding the best answers to these questions is likely to mean implicating a 'trials team' of managers (many of whom may only have a very small time involvement with the project).

Clearly one single 'project manager' is needed; for maximum success a 'champion' is needed also (see 'Championing and beyond' following); and in all probability some external 'partners', eg the telephone service providers, equipment providers and so on. Many of the potential external partners will publish advice on flexible working implementations: inevitably some do it well, some badly, and opinions on that must necessarily be somewhat subjective. That being said, the publications available from 3Com[1] are undoubtedly among the best of their type: they are totally American in style and content, but they are also based on real experience. 3Com did what every technical company should do and implemented flexible working in their own company using their own products. Unusually (and perhaps uniquely) 3Com then brutally publicised the shortcomings of their own equipment for the purpose, and set about remedying them. This reflects correctly the attitude in the opening sentence of this chapter — 'How best can we make this work?' The following extract from 3Com's excellent *Smart Valley Telecommuting Guide*[1] identifies the personnel you will need for a 'trials team'.

> *Establish a telecommuting implementation committee or team. As the flexible working project manager, you are responsible for putting the team together. Solicit the participation of the following people, or if you are part of a smaller organisation, account for these issues:*
>
> **Chief executive officer/chief operating officer/chief administrative officer**
>
> The actual CEO does not need to be directly involved with each implementation step; however, a representative from the CEO's office should be on the committee. Having access to this individual will provide an avenue for information to the highest ranking and most influential officer in the organisation.
>
> **Legal counsel**
>
> The legal representative of your organisation is responsible for reviewing and customising the flexible working agreement you

have chosen. If you decide to use a 'memo of understanding', your legal counsel needs to provide input for that document.

Human resources/training

The human resources department is responsible for developing a flexible working policy for the organisation. They may take responsibility for measuring the productivity of the employees selected to participate in the programme. They may also oversee the development of training material for telecommuters and their supervisors.

Labour relations

A labour relations representative is essential when working with union contracts. If your telecommuters are represented by unions it is critical to have the labour relations department involved with your implementation committee. They may choose to interact directly with the union or advise you to include a union representative or steward on your implementation team. They can also clarify flexible working responsibilities for management.

Ordinances/regulations

The transportation system manager or employee transportation co-ordinator should be on the implementation team. If your organisation must comply with transportation or air quality regulations, flexible working is a way to reduce the number of cars needed to conduct company business.

Emergency preparedness/disaster recovery

The business contingency planning co-ordinator may have an interest in the flexible working programme as a means of emergency preparedness planning. Flexible working on a regular basis can assist your organisation in preparing for emergencies.

Telecommunications/information systems

The telecommunications manager of your organisation must be included on your committee. The telecommunications department is responsible for supporting flexible working with the appropriate technology to be used at their remote locations.

Information systems will assist you with computer and software recommendations and can provide the team with information regarding data security.

Public relations

Flexible working will have a positive impact on your organisation. The public relations department will want to extol the virtues of the programme, both internally and externally.

All departments

Once the plan is designed, select participants for a pilot programme. A prototype is usually most successful when several different departments participate. If representatives from all of these departments are on the implementation team, you should have no difficulty finding participants for the pilot programme.

Championing and beyond

As with all change introduction processes, flexible working trials are more likely to have a successful outcome if there is proactive support at board level, ie if the project has a 'champion'. Assuming that there is board level support, the main blocking activity in an organisation is likely to come from middle management: those workers wishing to be involved will be actively in favour, those workers not wishing to be involved will be passive, but there will often be line managers who see only the risk of failure being laid at their door, without any upside benefit. Part of the 'championing' process must therefore be to ensure that management are fully on-side for the trial: the more senior the champion, the more the middle-management people will feel protected against the risk of failure.

Programming

These internal 'hearts and minds' activities dominate the early stages of a teleworking trial: the rest of the programme is rather more as you might expect from the preceding chapters:

Activity	Content
1	Strategy review and board level champion.
2	Management briefing and evangelising.
3	Task review and selection (Chapter 3).
4	Staff briefing and selection (Chapter 4).
5	Location review and selection (Chapter 5).

6 Equipment and faculties review and procurement (Chapter 6).
7 Institute training and briefing for flexible work teams (Chapter 7).
8 Create trial review and evaluation process (thischapter).
9 Make detail arrangements with flexible work teams (Chapter 7).
10 Start the trial and continuous evaluation.

Typically these activities might occupy a twelve-month period thus:

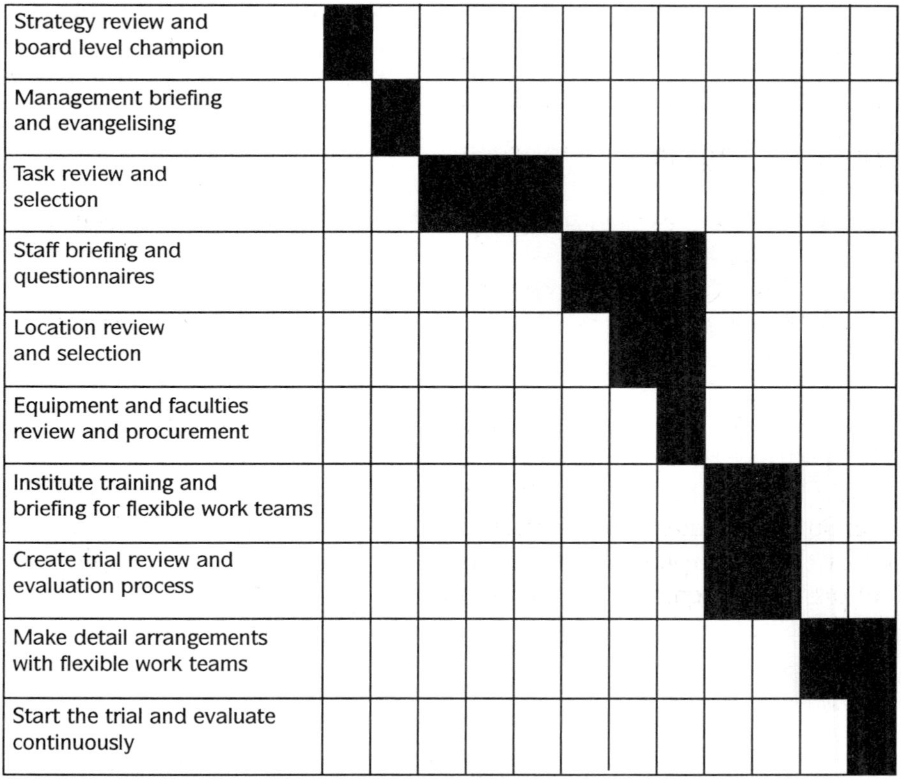

Ideally a flexible working trial should be intended to be of indefinite length, only being terminated in the unlikely event of failure. Evaluation is a topic that has to be considered very early on, prior to commencement. The first questions are those of why the trial is being undertaken:

- to demonstrate that flexible working is right for the business;

- to evaluate whether or not flexible working is right for the business;
- to assess which parts of the business might best benefit from flexible working;
- to measure the potential benefits of flexible working to check against other systems;
- to kick-start flexible working in the business.

Any or all of these reasons might operate: in practice they will affect the actual conduct of a trial only marginally, but it may be hard to claim success for a trial if there was no clear agreement at the outset on its objectives. The probability is that a trial's main objective will be concerned in some way with overcoming perceived obstacles to the introduction of flexible work, as much as with highlighting its benefits. In the *TELDET* survey of 2500 businesses throughout Europe, the main perceived obstacles were as shown in Figures 8.1 and 8.2[2].

Even where adverse issues have not specifically been raised as yet, it is clearly prudent for an evaluation process to look at these factors to counter subsequent criticism. This must involve a degree of benchmarking against the *status quo* (and also, where possible, against know norms for the industry or sector as a whole.)

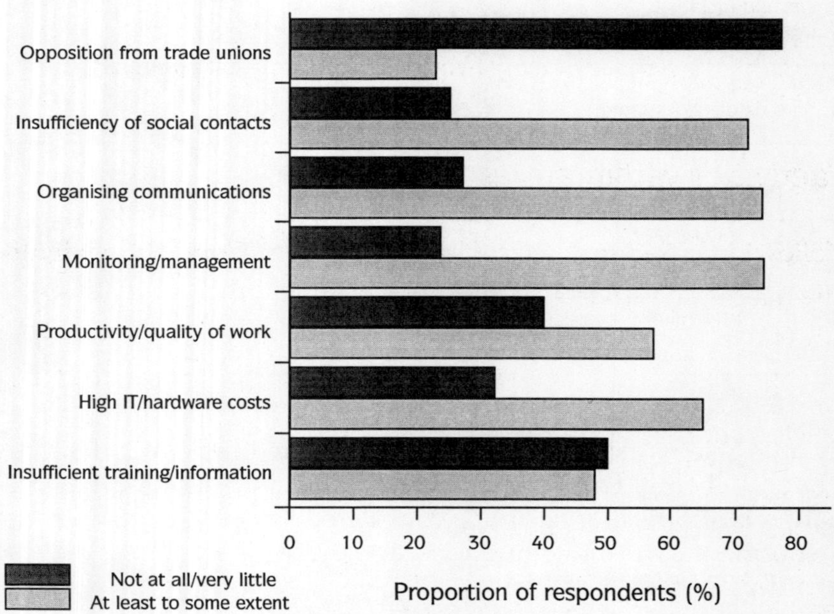

Figure 8.1 *Perceived obstacles to flexible working — employers' views*

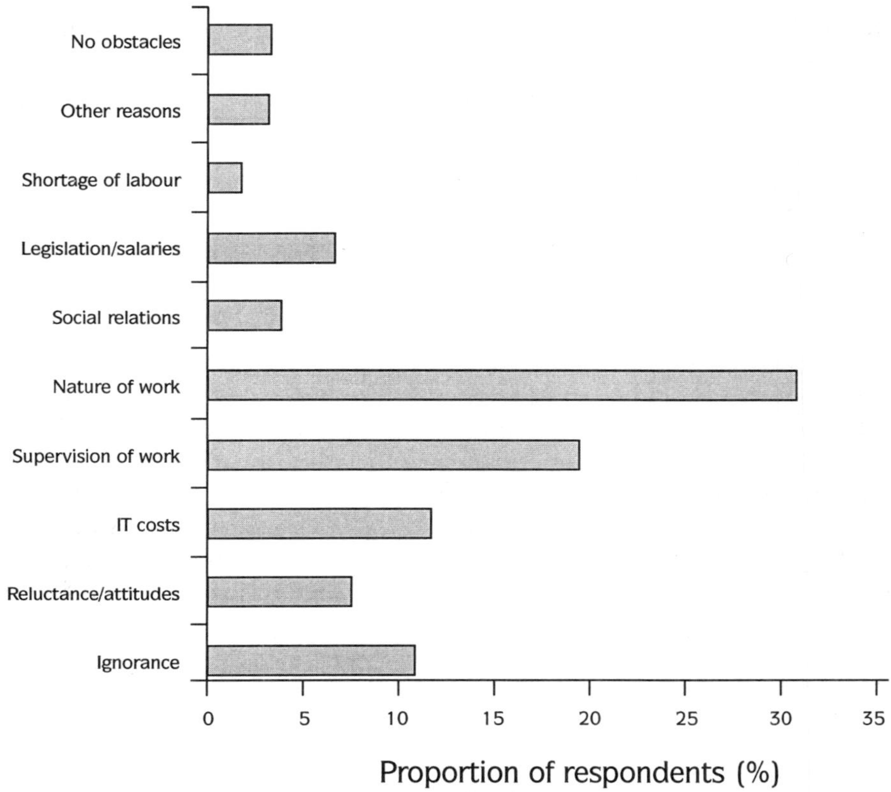

Figure 8.2 *Perceived obstacles to flexible working — employees' views*

The activities within a trial

The following boxed text, again drawn from the 3Com guide[1] identifies the main things that a trial should achieve.

> **Sell the programme constantly.** Clear understanding and constant promotion of the benefits of flexible working are essential. By managing the project you will acquire a global perspective. Share that perspective regularly, and emphasise the positive aspects of flexible working.
>
> **Get out the vote.** Spread the word about flexible working. Be creative and use every available means of communication. Promotional posters and banners are an effective way to let

employees know what is going on. Fliers can be distributed throughout the company mail system. These steps will help ensure that everyone understands why flexible working has been implemented in your organisation.

Pursue and promote a champion of flexible working. If your company has a department currently using flexible working to meet specialised business needs, encourage that department to join the effort in formalising flexible working for the whole organisation. They can become a control group to evaluate the success of your programme.

Emphasise the impact of flexible working on the environment. Explain to your organisation that air quality is a major concern and that flexible working is an effective way to reduce air pollution as well as an important strategy in complying with new air quality legislation.

Become the subject-matter expert. Become involved with flexible working professional* associations. Keep your eyes and ears open for all information pertaining to flexible working and how it is being used around the world.

Provide vision. Flexible working is an educational process. Resistance may exist because of a lack of understanding. Be aware of the changing needs of your working environment and how flexible working can meet those needs. Be creative in developing new flexible working applications for your organisation.

Support a voluntary programme. It is essential that the supervisors and telecommuters *volunteer* to participate in the programme. Do not force an employee who doesn't enjoy being at home to stay at home and work. Not everyone in your organisation will want to participate. Explaining the benefits carefully to prospective telecommuters enables them to make an educated choice.

Encourage part-time flexible working. The most successful prototype programmes have telecommuters working remotely one or two days a week. Very few individuals can successfully

* Note: Professional associations within the UK include:

National Association of Teleworkers, The Island House, Midsomer Norton, Bath, Avon BA3 2HL. Tel: 01761 413869; Fax: 01761 419348; C'serve: 100063,462.

DTI Telework Special Interest Group (TSIG), Peter Thomson, 212 Piccadilly, London W1V 9LD. Tel: 0171 917 2920; Fax: 0171 917 2836; E-mail: telework-request@mailbase.ac.uk.

stay at home five days a week. Complete isolation from the office has inherent drawbacks which should be avoided.

Determine an administrative structure. The flexible working implementation committee can help decide how the programme is to be administered. If the company is a large organisation, a flexible working co-ordinator could be appointed in each department to interface directly with the flexible working project manager. The co-ordinators would have decentralised positions, managing the flexible working programme in specific departments. Smaller organisations may want to conduct a centralised programme with a single project manager.

Establish a timeline. It is imperative to have a plan. This is a task for the flexible working implementation committee. The group can identify activities and assign responsible parties to complete them. All activities must have an assigned completion date. When building the timeline, understand that life is unpredictable. Be flexible enough to allow for dates to be changed. Encouraging everyone to participate in the process will afford ownership and accountability to your prototype programme.

Assist in formulating policy. Large organisations will have many people involved in policy formation. In a small organisation, this activity may be the responsibility of one person. Whatever size your organisation is, design a policy which allows flexibility and freedom for individual customisation.

Assume a leadership role in the selection process. Your organisation will require guidance in selecting the telecommuters and supervisors to participate in the pilot programme. Provide insight to the implementation committee regarding selection criteria. Also, encourage the participants to use the selection survey process developed for the organisation.

Provide input regarding training requirements. You, the flexible working project manager will know best what subjects should be covered during the training sessions. Be sure to address the requirements for supervisors, telecommuters and office-based employees.

Identify safety considerations. The implementation team should provide input regarding safety. If your organisation has a safety policy, you may be able to enhance the current policy to encompass flexible working issues. If you don't have a safety policy, flexible working could be a catalyst for the development of one.

Determine and recommend support materials. The pilot programme will need specific reference material to support it. It is recommended that a flexible working manual or a guide be provided to assist the telecommuters when getting started.

Assist in determination of equipment policy. Your organisation will need an equipment provision policy. Large organisations can delegate those decisions to the individual groups or departments. Small organisations can develop one equipment policy with which everyone complies.

Steward the evaluation efforts. The success of a programme cannot be determined without evaluation. It is critical for everyone participating in the pilot programme to participate in the evaluation. The implementation committee can devise the criteria for measuring progress and ultimately, the success of the programme.

Practise what you preach. You need to work at least one day a week at home in order to obtain first-hand experience about flexible working. Assign time on your own calendar for regular flexible working.

Provide status reports to upper management. The implementation committee needs to identify milestones and benchmarks for the programme. Both general progress and individual participation should be monitored. The resulting information can be shared with senior management in the form of a progress report.

Form a telecommuters' support group. Telecommuters can develop a networking group or forum to share their experiences. The organisation does not have to provide the time to participate in these forums; telecommuters can meet at lunch or before or after work.

Fine-tune the programme. Be flexible enough to make changes when and where necessary. Be prepared to share the success!

A checklist for teleworking trials

These checklists are numbered according to the outline programme in the previous section 'Programming', activities 1–10.

Strategy review (activity 1)

- Does flexible working fit into your corporate strategy?
  - What is the strategy for introducing teleworking?
  - What is the strategy for extending teleworking?
- Can your management structure adapt to flexible working?
- What are the potential commercial benefits?
  - productivity gains;
  - more flexible working hours (= improved customer service);
  - retention of skilled employees (= lower recruitment and training costs);
  - wider recruitment opportunities;
  - elimination of relocation costs.
- Is there support from senior management?

Management briefing and evangelism (activity 2)

- Analysis of information flows, business processes and work patterns.
- What benefits would staff enjoy?
  - more flexible working hours;
  - reduced commuting time/cost/stress;
  - fewer interruptions;
  - greater freedom to organise working environment;
  - reduced commuting;
  - less traffic congestion;
  - reduced pollution;
  - lower demand for city-centre offices;
  - greater demand for space in homes or telecentres.
- How will they see the company benefit?
  - more competitive;
  - long-term survival.

Task review and selection (activity 3)

- What jobs are suitable for flexible working?
  - major computer users (eg accounts administration);
  - major telephone users (eg customer support staff);
  - mobile workers (eg sales representatives).

Staff briefing and selection (activity 4)

- What categories of staff adapt well to flexible working?
  - — familiar with existing company procedures;
  - — self-motivated;
  - — able to work without constant supervision.

What technology will flexible workers need? (activity 6)

- Information technology (eg PCs with Windows applications).
- Telecommunications (eg ISDN lines).
- Multi-media (eg desk-top video-conferencing).
- Changed telecommunications requirements (eg new PABX).
- Changes to PC/LAN environment (eg remote access).
- New technology (eg document image processing).

Trial review and evaluation (activity 8)

- Cost/benefit analysis.
- Evaluation of benefits in absolute terms and in relation to other trials.
- Employee/management reactions.
- Interim reports quarterly.
- Full report after 12 months.
- Recommendations for future action.

Detail arrangements with teams (activity 9)

- Potential loss of managerial control.
- Potential reduction in quality of work.
- Security of data.
- Social isolation.
- Reduced motivation (perceived lack of promotion prospects).
- Increased cost of telecommunications.
- Legal and regulatory hurdles.

- Can video replace face-to-face meetings with managers and colleagues?
- Should flexible workers still attend regular office meetings?
- Would the use of a remote telecentre be appropriate?
- Would a new telecommunications system reduce costs?

Evaluation (activity 10)

- What are the expected benefits?
- Outline cost/benefit analysis.
- Implement the project plan.
- Collect data on productivity, costs, quality of work, etc.
- Monitor employee and management attitudes.
- Provide necessary additional training (use of a help desk).
- Change computer or communications equipment if required.

Chapter 9

Beyond the trial — the longer-term future

The flexible future

Most business decisions are based on a prediction of the future, or at least necessitate one's having first come to a clear view of, or plan for, the future. Views of the future tend to be based either on a cautious extrapolation of the past and present ('we sold 6000 last year and 7000 this so let's assume 7500–8000 for next year') or wish-fulfilment ('next year we're really going to make it'): each of these methods has its value. Extrapolation from the past is particularly valuable for assessing the immediate short-term future, but runs increasingly into problems as it is extended ever further forward, because the errors build up exponentially: this is particularly damaging in situations of rapid change, when the future looks little like the past. For middle-term planning, many large organisations now use the technique of developing a full statement of where they wish (or intend, or dream!) to be in, say, ten years' time, and then predict next year's situation by interpolating backwards from the longer term. Technically, this has the benefit of having a single and assessable source of error, (the long-term scenario itself) so that the errors build up linearly, not exponentially as in the more common extrapolation method. On the other hand, the risk of getting the long view hopelessly wrong is all too evident, which is why I referred to this as the wish-fulfilment (rather than the fantasy) method: it works best, when the plan is in fact a statement of serious intent, carried through vigorously and with commitment. Knowing where you want to go, and wanting it seriously, rather obviously increases your likelihood of being able to get there.

There is more to the wish-fulfilment method than mere self-help homily, however: you and your organisation can, to some extent, shape the future to comply with what you want, but so too can everyone else. This then begins to give a viable method of predicting the future, by looking at wants and needs, and at the possibilities of fulfilling those wants and needs. Technology changes and new products are very visibly tied to wants and needs by market forces, and so too are changes in the pattern of work and flexible working. Some of the wants and needs are corporate, producing changes that tend to be categorised within the business process re-engineering area of flexible working, and some of the wants and needs are individual, and produce changes that tend to be categorised within the teleworking area of flexible working.

More action for less money

In the 50-year period 1944 to 1994, a quite astonishing geometrical progression occurred in the power/price ratio for IT products, following what is known as the 'Triple-Ten Law': every ten years, the power of IT equipment in use increased tenfold, and like-for-like its price decreased to one-tenth. This gives a pretty astonishing change in 'bangs-per-buck' in those 50 years: today's equipment is 10^5 times as cost-effective as that of 1949 (that is 100,000 times as powerful per pound of cost). In simple terms, what cost £100 million then, costs £1000 now: a commonplace desktop PC of today, equates in power to the whole of the defence industry's total computer power then.

This sort of history makes looking forward by even a few years seem quite terrifying: extending forward 50 years on this sort of numeric basis, corner grocery stores would be putting their own satellites in orbit to take orders for cartons of milk. In building up a view of the likely future for your business, a more useful way of looking at the growth phenomenon is to realise that information technology hardware will assuredly become so cheap, that its price will no longer be any restraint at all to even small businesses. Fifty years ago, cars were strictly for the wealthy: now almost every small business uses at least one car. The guiding principle here is that, if what you want or need represents a commonplace want or need for a sufficiently large number of people, then in the future, fulfilment of that want or need is going to be very cheap. Mercury Communications expect all telephone call charges for other than international calls to be free by the year 2005 (the income Mercury needs will come from providing value-added services, not from boring old call charges). That does not involve only simple old copper wire telephones: fibre-optic will also cost next to nothing, so bandwidth will become cheap and commonplace (but remember that, in real terms, UK phone costs 'only' dropped 38 per cent from 1990–1995 — there will be no rush towards financial suicide by the telephone companies). For planning purposes, however, it is possible to assume very low costs indeed for communications over a ten-year timescale. Also, even if tariffs drop only slowly, the cost per bit carried will drop much faster for data, as transmission speeds increase, and as faster modems, ISDN adapters and services at higher rates than ISDN, come into common use. The Triple-Ten Law obviously cannot go on for ever, but it does seem still to have some steam left for the next few years.

Sciomorphs

When technology changes first come in, people mostly do not know what to do with them for the best, so they start out by emulating exactly the same old things that they used to do. Predicting the future for flexible work methods necessitates thinking about totally new tasks being done in totally new ways, and forgetting about just doing the same old tasks (albeit in better ways).

The classic (literally) example of this hanging on to old ways of thinking is the *sciomorph* (lit. ghost-form) of Greek architecture: when the new technology of building in stone started to replace the old technology of building in wood, stone lintels (over door and window openings) were initially cut to exactly the same shapes and sizes as the old timber ones, and this habit went on for many decades, until the new shapes utilising and reflecting the strength of stone rather than of wood created the architecture that we still admire today. Much of our existing commonplace business administration is sciomorphic; still retaining old habits that made sense in a pre-microchip world, but no longer having meaning today.

It is particularly important to avoid such sciomorphs in flexible working — for example, sending out paper order forms (submitted by a company's representatives) to a homeworker to key into an ordering system. This may indeed be a step forward from the old way of employing someone in the office to do the job: there may be a money saving, possibly, but this system is nonetheless sciomorphic — what is being done is the same old task, just in a slightly more flexible way. Looking to the future might first involve asking what the representative is doing with paper forms when he could have a notebook PC — but even this is still sciomorphic. More radical thinking would lead to wondering why the representative sends in the customer's orders at all:

- Is the customer adult?
- Does the customer really want to have to wait until the rep calls?
- Why is your business not empowering the customer to trigger actions in your business directly?
- Why is the works not handling its own orders?

If you are thinking strategically about the future, do not be held back by the past. A better flexible working response in this case might be to assign the sales representative to work with the customer directly, handling procurement of products on a teleworking basis, and avoiding paper totally. (Incidentally transforming the representatives premises overhead costs directly to the customer, instead of hiding them in the cost of orders.)

Foreseeable radical changes

Businesses as people

Even without the influence of flexible working methods, there are strong pressures for structural change in businesses in developed countries. One major theme in this pressure for change is the concept of stakeholding (as opposed to shareholding) in a business. Even the lowliest of employees in a business is a stakeholder, having a real interest in the welfare of the business, and being inevitably bound up in it. People matter, and their importance will be much more visible in flexible work businesses which inevitably tend to have high information (as opposed to product) content.

Flexible working methods, properly implemented, can be very empowering to employees, but in ways that challenge the old 'company man' concept of the unthinkingly loyal manager supporting the business, right or wrong. New loyalties (to projects, to teams and to professional excellence) will come up alongside the old company loyalties, and will in their turn create new motivations for stakeholders. At first glance, this loosening of ties can be a frightening prospect for businesses: their once-loyal staff will cease to be company people and become flexible people, quite possibly even moving backwards and forwards between competing businesses as work ebbs and flows. This will need new techniques to motivate the staff, but the concept of stakeholding, added to:

- improvements in working conditions;
- less damage to family/marriage/relationships;
- better utilisation of skills among female staff;
- better use of temporary and part-time staff;

will itself generate new loyalties and new enthusiasms. There will always be gloom-mongers to talk down flexible work, but the reality is of something which has proved to be popular with staff and good for businesses, and that can be expected to continue.

The office as a café

Café society has always been popular in Europe, and also has been much associated with doing business (Lloyds, for instance, was originally a café). Many of the more advanced models of flexible work (as outlined in Chapter 5) are reverting to this seventeenth century model of the workplace as a place where friends meet. This has implications for the locations of offices, particularly implying that they should move closer to transport centres such as airports or motorway intersections. These new offices look quite like hotels, and operate in a hotel-like fashion (rent a room for the day, for instance), so finding them in the same locations that attract hotels is not a surprise, and neither should be the possibility that their management eventually will be outsourced to hotel operators.

Two simultaneous streams of change carry this evolution along: on the one hand, business is moving from an era of desktop PC dominance to one of communications dominance; on the other hand, facilities management is increasingly a concept tied to outsourcing. The outcome is not just a move away from fixed overheads and extraneous capital use, it is also a real blurring of the distinction between hotel and office, which is reflected also in the blurring of other similar distinctions. Homes may become offices, but so too will hotels, restaurants, cafés and even copy shops, at the same time destroying the hard and fast distinction between work and leisure. The Cyber Café may prove to be just a passing phase, but the café as a place of work is a very enduring concept.

Work as play

The Balearic Islands of Spain have an autonomous regional government (Govern Balear) which has a total commitment to flexible work as the shape of the future. Realising that flexible work tends to destroy the distinction between work and 'not-work', they are moving actively to destroy also the distinctions between work and holiday, and between work and retirement.

In a flexible work business, international boundaries will tend rather quickly to become an irrelevance (albeit remaining a great nuisance). Domicile then also ceases to be a concept for anything other than taxation, and the business is where its stakeholders are. Stakeholders who have no fixed geographical ties are most likely to go to one of two types of area — first, where they were born; and second, exceptionally pleasant areas. The first effect is simply dispersive, but the second will inevitably move businesses to holiday areas like the Balearics (or the Sophia Antopolis development in the South of France). UK holiday regions may benefit to some extent, if they wake up in time, but these go-ahead regions in Spain and France have achieved great success already by establishing science parks within minutes of the beach, by establishing conference holidays as a technique to merge work seamlessly into enjoyment, and by setting out to attract semi-retired stakeholders of flexible businesses to relocate, and so to merge work seamlessly into retirement.

There is an élitism about all this which can be downright offensive to those brought up on a factory-based work ethic of decent toil and salt of the earth; this distinction between the 'us' who are information based, PC and communication literate, flexible and successful, and the 'them' who are none of those, represents both the main reason for implementing flexible work and, potentially, its worst drawback.

Post-materialism

Curiously, in all these future developments, money (or rather remuneration) becomes much less of an issue. Quality of life is what will be brought by flexible working, not standard of living (ie consumerism). Given that the current number of information workers (ie potential flexible workers) in the world is between 600 million and 700 million, with 30 per cent of that number within Organization for Economic Co-operation and Development (OECD) countries, this is a major potential change area. To have 600 million workers becoming more interested in quality of life than in raw earnings would represent a truly shattering change in the structure of society.

Running in parallel with this is the greater population growth in non-OECD countries, and also the tendency for new technologies (like flexible working) to migrate down the skills scale (for instance into call centre and telesales operations). This all means that OECD area businesses which are implementing flexible working today in order to stay competitive with other OECD businesses, will find themselves having to sharpen-up the efficiency of their flexible working very greatly in the next decade in order to stay competitive with non-OECD (Third World) countries.

Post-Fordism

Staying competitive with Third World countries as they develop will yet further modify flexible working into something more analogous to assembly line manufacturing. Specialist units (call centres) will handle the customer and supplier interface, ie both incoming and outgoing calls. Call centres will have no particular geographic bias, so they will become a location independent, industry independent sector on their own. Naturally this will tend also to be an edge-of-town, trading estate type activity for its facilities provision. Add to this the change, already described, in office facilities to being drop-in centres at transport hubs, run by hotel specialists, and the future for the city-centre real estate market looks bleak. Until, that is, you recall that people actually often like to live in city centres and were only driven out from them by insane real estate values fuelled by office use. The future may well see some premises handling the same work tasks as in the past, but now in the guise of home offices, having been converted to domestic dwellings.

Tomorrow's technologies

Chapter 6 discussed the immediately foreseeable changes in technologies in detail, but it is also necessary to keep half an eye on the less easily foreseeable longer term. More bandwidth and more speed seem to be more or less guaranteed to figure in future changes. The move from 'linear text' to 'simultaneous pictures', must also eventually mean far more sophisticated input devices, such as voice activation and presumably eventually the use of smart video/audio cameras and microphones. Such changes have massive impacts on the size of 'files' and hence on network traffic. A single page A4 document prepared on a text processor in say 1985 was about 2Kb of data; the same content prepared on a Windows word processor in 1995 might occupy 40Kb; but in 2005, with audio and video clip inclusions, it might well grow to 20Mb — increasing by a factor of 10,000 in 20 years.

Such huge increases in content, coupled with huge increases in the number of users, will almost certainly see the end of copper wire transmission, and indeed can be expected to put fibre-optic under strain. Broadcast networks must therefore come more into prominence. At the same time, as more different networks come into use, a new generation of switches, bridges and routers will develop very rapidly to give seamless, transparent operation. Many different network topographies exist and are proposed, but users are only interested in one sort. This network could be described as a sort of blanket, covering the whole world, with two pins sticking out of it: you and the person to whom you are talking. The old-fashioned PSTN telephone already looks like that, and it can reasonably be expected that in ten years or so all communications networks will have converged into that blanket topography.

Tomorrow's businesses

Changing the way that business is done is a benefit arising from flexible working, but the most effective benefits will come from changing the business that is done not from changing how it is done (see the earlier section on 'Sciomorphs'). Wholly new businesses will arise which are:

- Loosely located — the domicile of the business will move along with its stakeholders.
- Loosely defined — the personnel of the business will come and go on a 'project' basis, often to and from competitors.
- Widely informed — drawing on many data sources including voice, hand-written script, sketches, video clips and television.
- Proactively run — near-instant access to people and to data will allow much quicker and more intuitive management.
- Trading in new 'stuff' — dealing in entities which either did not exist before or were never regarded as 'stuff' to trade: the new info-businesses.

Making the reasonable assumption that Third World countries in the future will become highly competitive against even flexible working developed world conventional businesses, then the best future for the developed world must be in wholly new types of business. Some of these are outlined in Chapter 1 but they will include at least the following:

- Tele-medicine.
- Distance-learning and tele-education.
- On-line entertainment and media.
- Real time on-line gambling.
- Real time information services.
- Electronic publishing including electronic distribution.
- Night market business services.
- Charging and billing for goods and services as an industry sector on its own.
- Data mining, extraction, refining, recycling, disposal and security services.
- Brokering and trading in real and virtual goods and services.
- Digital imaging and photography.
- Virtual museums and galleries.
- Virtual zoos, wildlife experiences.
- Virtual reality experiences, eg flying, diving, parachuting.
- Electronic sports and competitions.
- Tele-travel and virtual reality tourism.

Publishing new 'stuff'...

Publishing extended away from its paper base in several jumps: the phonograph was one jump, and was followed quickly by copyright extension into recorded musical performances. Still and moving photography had similar histories. Radio and then television were further jumps with further extensions to copyright law following them, and in due course disk-based software made another jump, both in widening the bounds of publishing and in extending copyright law. The jump represented by E-mail and the Internet poses real problems in intellectual property rights, which are as yet unresolved. This is in part a philosophical difficulty: different digitised images of the *Mona Lisa* at different standards will differ materially from one another and from the original, so any copyright would logically go to the 'digitiser', just as it would to the photographer in still photography. However, digitising and then marginally modifying images is phenomenally easy, and their wide-spread publication virtually instantaneous, so the other part of the problem is the sheer ease of plagiarism.

As a result, possibly billions of pounds worth of intellectual property is currently being traded globally each year without the accrual of copyright, and often also without the imposition of local or national taxation or of customs duties. The Internet in particular looks uncomfortably like Dodge City before the arrival of the first Sheriff. Clearly new business opportunities arise here, both 'grey' (plagiarism based publishing, data theft, 'tax-free' trading, and so on) and 'white' (monitoring and auditing, encryption, electronic policing, tax and excise functions and so on).

... and avoiding 'publication'

For every £1 of turnover generated in electronic publishing, there may well be another in 'privacy' services. For both individuals and businesses, their habits of behaviour; purchasing; travelling; communications; work; and even social relationships potentially will be available for analysis by the electronic eavesdropper. A few individuals and businesses will become 'drop-outs', using aliases and subterfuge to avoid this sort of analysis, but most will be open to being 'sold' privacy services that will ring-fence them from intrusion in the same way that policing and security services do today to secure physical privacy.

As the volume of statistical data grows, so measures like the Data Protection Act will become progressively less meaningful, simply because it will be implausible to locate every single item of data about an individual or business, let alone download it for checking. Already 'grey' services exist to 'clear' debt judgements, for instance: providing sanitised data to overlay the truth may extend the scope of the public relations industry into virtually every individual home, and certainly will extend to most businesses. At this stage, anarchy looms as it becomes impossible to distinguish fact from fiction — but doubtless there were those who said that of the printing press.

Brave new world

Eventually, therefore, it is necessary to adopt a sort of unthinking optimism about it all, and to recall what was said at the beginning of this Chapter about predicting the future in terms of wants and needs. For most businesses, the least known aspect of the future is 'What do we want from it?' If any sort of resolution of that is available, then the future can be faced with confidence.

Appendix A

The trade union view

A trade union perspective on flexible working

This essay on the trade union view is reprinted, by permission of the publishers, from *The European Journal of Teleworking,* Volume 1 Number 4, 1993. Its author, Bill Walsh, is Regional Officer with the Manufacturing, Science and Finance (MSF) Union, a home-based flexible worker himself, and the leading UK authority on this subject. ✓

For many the daily journey to and from work by public transport is lengthy and expensive and often very unpleasant. Those who opt to use their own transport hardly fare better.

The existing framework of the labour market imprisons many people and excludes others at the same time. Its rigidity is an unattractive feature of modern life, putting people and their needs very much in second place to the needs of the businesses which employ them. Flexible working offers the opportunity to review this and to provide a range of options from which the individuals could choose. On the wider scale, fewer offices and commuters, less general movement of the population to and from workplaces, could have considerable benefits for the environment and the local economies of many so-called 'dormitory' towns and villages around the country.

Suspicion

For all this, trade unionists are deeply suspicious of any extension of home-based working. There is a long and discreditable history of, as well as ongoing, exploitation of home workers. The clothing industry is just one example of a sector employing thousands of people on a subcontract basis to turn out goods in their own homes for a tiny fraction of their real value. While recognising the potential to liberalise the labour market, many point to employers as being responsible for the rigidity of the current workplace and are scornful of the idea that they will be interested in liberating people from it. Instead they believe that a home working environment will be even more of a prison. Lastly, and above all, they believe that employers will use home-based working to drive down costs at the expense of the wages and other conditions of employment of conventional employees, to isolate individuals, destroy collective organisation and that the widespread exploitation that goes with traditional home working will go with flexible working as well.

Our union, the Manufacturing, Science and Finance Union, has no illusions about this. There are good and bad employers and there will be those who will use the new technologies to offer new services to businesses and who will employ people on poor pay and in unsatisfactory conditions, without safeguards. However, for trades unions, a knee jerk reaction based on the experience of worst cases is not a sufficient response. Nor does it indicate the confidence that trades unionists should feel, on the basis of their record, of being able to negotiate and campaign for the protection that people might need in these new circumstances. The alternative to taking a positive stance on these potential developments, is to try to sustain the unsatisfactory and unpopular employment *status quo* for many people who will want to opt for change, and trades unions will find that employers — and even worse — many of their members, will simply ignore them and come to terms on their own account.

For these reasons, MSF is campaigning to ensure that home-based working is a genuine extension of freedom for people at work and that it does not become a lonely prison for men and women who are unable, for family reasons or because of disability, to attend a more traditional workplace and who cannot, therefore, participate or compete in the labour market. The union wants to see a wide range of employment opportunities made available to the home-based teleworker, and not just low paid routine tasks, which carry no career prospects.

Choice

We want to see home-based work offered as an alternative for people to choose and not an imposed revision of existing arrangements. In all circumstances employers should consult with their staff and negotiate contracts with them and their representatives. We welcome the emphasis placed on this process by both British Telecom and Mercury in the teleworking guides which they have produced.

Beyond this and in the current unregulated UK labour market, MSF believes that there is sufficient protection included in the discussions taking place in the European Commission about the application of the Social Charter, as well as arguing for changes in domestic UK regulations.

MSF has produced a checklist for negotiating home based teleworking arrangements with employers. The main points are:

- Home-based working should always be voluntary.
- Home-based workers should be employees (enjoying full employment rights) and not self-employed subcontractors.
- Ideally, home-based teleworking should operate from a separate room in the home examined by qualified health and safety experts to ensure a safe working environment.
- There should be regular opportunities for teleworkers in the same organisation to meet each other, as well as non-teleworking colleagues and managers, so that people do not feel isolated and excluded.
- Teleworkers should have access to electronic mail and telephone links with each other — using the scope of the technology to expand contact between people and further avoid isolation.
- Each teleworker should be assigned a particular manager whose responsibility it should be to keep in regular contact and meet the teleworker on a regular basis.
- Teleworkers should enjoy the same rates of pay and other employment benefits as non teleworking employees in an organisation.
- Teleworkers should be included in the career development programme of the organisation in which they work.
- All equipment used should be supplied and maintained by the employer.
- Financial arrangements should be agreed to cover the extra costs of teleworking, such as heating, lighting, etc, and it also may be appropriate for a rental to be agreed for the use made of an employee's home.
- Employers should be responsible for the health and safety of teleworkers and have special health and safety advisers to give advice and regularly to visit and monitor health and safety.

- Teleworkers should be represented, through their own employee representatives, on health and safety committees of the organisations that employ them.
- Teleworkers should enjoy the same rights as other workers to join trades unions and should have access to representatives, including the right to elect their own. In this regard, trades unions will need to think about the services that they may need to offer teleworkers, including access to electronic mail, notice boards etc.
- Employees who transfer from conventional based working to home-based teleworking should be entitled to a trial period and should have the right to return to the previous arrangements. All teleworkers should have an annual review of the arrangements and the right to revert to the previous arrangements if they wish.

Beyond these points, to which we would expect to get agreement by employers, MSF believes that legal safeguards are required for the protection of people. We are campaigning for the following:

1. The strengthening of health and safety legislation specifically to cover all home-based workers and for the health and safety executive to have a homeworker inspectorate.
2.. A legal right for teleworkers to have access to information about the pay and conditions of other teleworkers in an organisation.
3. The establishment of a legal right — with appropriate remedies — to refuse to work from home.
4. The outlawing of 'waiver' clauses that would deprive teleworkers of legal rights.

Appendix B

References

Chapter 1

1. Empirica (D) IDATE(F) Work Research Centre (Irl) INMARK (E) and INNOVA (I) (1995) *TELDET: Final Report of the TELDET Project* (Project T1016 of the EC DGXIII-B), Empirica, Oxfordstrasse-2, D53111, Bonn, Fax: +49 228 98530 12, E-mail: WERNER@EMP-D.UUCP

2. Experteam Telecom(D) IDATE (F) *European Telecommunications Handbook for Teleworkers* (1994) (project T1022 of the EC DGXIII-B), Experteam Telecom, Dortmund, Fax: +49 231 7546 754

Chapter 2

1. Varcoe, B (1995) 'Times-Procord Office Costs Index', Published in *The Times*, 19 July, Times Newspapers Ltd, 1 Virginia St, London, E1 9XN, Tel: (UK) +44 (0)171 782 5000

2. Gray, M, Hodson, N and Gordon, G (1993) *Teleworking Explained*, John Wiley & Sons, Chichester, UK (ISBN D-471-93975-7)

3. *TELDET: Final Report of the TELDET Project*, Op cit as Chapter 1, number 1

4. Eldis, OE and Minoli, D (1995) *Telecommuting*, Artech House Inc, 685 Canton Street, Norwood, MA 02062, USA (ISBN 0-89006-738-4), Fax: (UK) +44 (0) 171 630 0166

Chapter 3

1. *TELDET: Final Report of the TELDET Project*, Op cit as Chapter 1, number 1
2. *European Telecommunications Handbook for Teleworkers*, Op cit as Chapter 1, number 2
3. Huws, U (1993) *Teleworking in Britain*, Research Paper 18, Research Management Branch, Department of Employment, Moorfoot, Sheffield S1 4PQ, Tel: +44 (0)1742 593932
4. Huws, U (1995) *A Manager's Guide to Teleworking*, The Employment Department, London, available from Cambortown Ltd, Unit 8, Goldthorpe Industrial Estate, Rotherham, South Yorkshire S63 9BL
5. Murray, B (1992) *Teleworking in the UK*, National Computing Centre (NCC) Ltd, Oxford Road, Manchester M1 7ED
6. Coulson-Thomas, C (1994) *Business Process Re-engineering — Myth and Reality*, Kogan Page, London (ISBN 0-7494-1442-1)

Chapter 4

1. Stanworth, C and Stanworth, J (1994) 'The social dimension' *The European Journal of Teleworking* 2(3), Addico Cornix Publications, 70 Causewayhead, Penzance, Cornwall TR18 2SR, Fax: +44 1736 69477 (ISSN 0966 7458) pp 4–8
2. Haddon, L (1994) 'Teleworking in the 1990s — a view from the home' *The European Journal of Teleworking* (details as number 1 above) Vol 2, no 3, pp 17–20
3. *A Manager's Guide to Teleworking*, Op cit as Chapter 3, number 4
4. Kinsman, F (co-author) *The Flexible Working Portfolio for Large Employee Organizations*, Mercury Communications Ltd (1992) New Mercury House, 26 Red Lion Square, London WC1R 4HQ, Freecall 0500 700 101
5. Bailyn, L (1988) *Towards the Perfect Workplace*, Sloan School of Management, Massachusetts Institute of Technology, Cambridge, MA, Sloan WP # 1993–88

6. Kakabadse, A, Ludlow, R and Vinnicombe, S (1987) *Working in Organizations*, Gower, Aldershot (1987) and Penguin Books, Harmondsworth (1988) (ISBN 0-009141-6)

Chapter 5

1. Health and Safety Executive (1995) *How to Deal with Sick Building Syndrome*, HSE Books, PO Box 1999, Sudbury, Suffolk CO10 6FS, Fax: +44 (0)1787 313995

Chapter 6

1. 'The Physicist' (Interview with Nathan Myhvrold), *Wired* 1(5) (UK edition) Wired, PO Box 960, 200 Aldergate Street, London EC1A 4HJ, Fax: +44 (0) 171 833 2957 (ISSN 1357-0978)
2. *Software and Hardware Sales in Europe* Authors Dataquest and the Software Publishers Association, Quoted in *The European*, 21–27 July 1995. Published by *The European*, 200 Gray's Inn Road, London WC1X 8NE, Fax: +44 (0) 171 713 1840.
3. 'LAN interconnection via ISDN' Authors Fischer and Lorenz; Tecsiel; and Ovum Ltd. Published by Ovum Ltd (1994) 1 Mortimer Street, London W1N 7RH, UK

Chapter 7

1. Buckman, B and Rowe, T (1992) *Training for Teleworking*, National Council of Educational Technology, Science Park, Sir William Lyons Road, Coventry CV4 7EZ (ISBN 1-85379-176-8)
2. 'The Social Dimension', Op cit as Chapter 4, number 1
3. *European Telecommunications Handbook for Teleworkers*, Op cit as Chapter 1, number 2
4. SyncNet, Product Details from PTT, Unit 5B Old Dairy Estate, Sancreed, Penzance, Cornwall TR20 8QP, Fax: +44 (0)1736 810160
5. *The Flexible Working Portfolio*, Op cit as Chapter 4, number 4

6. QMT Introduction Pack, National Association of Telework, The Island House, Midsomer Norton, Bath, Avon BA3 2HL, Fax: +44 (0) 1761 419348

Chapter 8

1. *3Com Smart Valley Telecommuting Guide*, 3Com Europe Limited, Wolsey Business Park, Tolpits Lane, Watford, Hertfordshire, WD1 8BL, Fax: +44 (0)1923 240446

2. *TELDET: Final Report of the TELDET Project*, Op cit as Chapter 1, number 1

Appendix C

Glossary

ATM: Asynchronous transfer mode is a new fast packet-switching technology potentially capable of switching all types of telecommunications traffic, and likely to be the leading technology of its type in the late 1990s.

Back office: The back office is becoming an increasingly popular concept with corporate organisations and large companies. The back office provides all the normal services of administration, secretarial etc, but from a remote location. This back office is usually a dedicated office building located in an area of lower cost. As pressure and the cost of operating large office space in city centres increases along with the environmental and cost factors involved in commuting, the back office concept is likely to become more common.

B-channel: The bearer channel in ISDN communication carries voice, data or video signals; a dial-up 64Kbits/s digital circuit.

BRI: The ISDN **basic rate interface** offers two B-channels and a D-channel.

Bridge: Networking device; a layer two network device which learns the addresses on its ports and only forwards packets across the bridge if the destination address is on the other side.

Broadband networks: High capacity, two-way communications technologies that support voice, data and video. A variety of technologies can support broadband, including ISDN.

Calling line identifier: The telephone number of the device originating a call.

CD-ROM: Compact disk: in the business context, a read-only storage medium taking 640Mb of digital data.

Cellular radio: The basis for mobile phones: uses a network of radio transmitters organised into cells, with adjacent cells broadcasting on different non-interfering frequencies, and with automatic switching between cells.

CIT: Computer integrated telephony: The interface between PABXs and computers. Applications include screen-based telephony call centres, desktop conferencing, whiteboarding etc.

Client server: An architecture where tasks are broken down to distributed processes, in which the client is responsible for the presentation of the information and the server for finding the required information.

Closed teleworking: Closed teleworking refers to teleworking which is carried out by a supplier of a service in close relationship with a client or clients. This form of telework is closed in the sense that the supplier is not actively marketing services on an open market basis. Many teleworkers are content with this form of working, but there are also many who move to a larger market or a more secure client base by offering their services in an open way — see **open teleworking**.

Compression: Reduction of the quantity of data needed to store and transmit information. Many standards exist, particularly the Mx series for modems, JPEG for still pictures and MPEG for video.

D-channel: The data channel in ISDN communication carries control and signalling information to set up and break down connections, primarily used for call set-up and management. Unlike the B-channels, it is a permanent connection.

Desktop Conferencing: Typically a Windows-based product which provides video conferencing, shared whiteboard and file transfer functions.

EDI: Electronic data interchange: The electronic communication of formally structured operational data (such as orders and invoices) between organisations.

E-mail: The store and forwarding of messages containing text, image, sound, video and programs using electronic transmission.

Ethernet: The most popular type of local area network. Devices wait until the LAN is quiet before transmitting. If two transmit at the same time, both hear the collision and wait a random period of time before re-sending. Originally 10Mbit/s, now has a 100Mbit/s option.

FDDI: Fibre distributed data interface, an alternative, 100Mbit/s LAN popular for campus networks.

GSM: Global system for mobile communication. A two-way, pan-European digital cellular system. (Used to be Groupe Service Mobile but that sounded too French for the UK market).

Hypertext: Highlighted text, image or icon which when clicked on takes the user to further related information (sound, text image, animation or video) on the same topic.

Internet: The world's largest network of more than 10,000 autonomous networks, based on the comparatively 'open' network protocol TCP/IP, and developed initially by the US Government. The usage of the Internet is increasing rapidly through new Internet service providers. The Internet has more than 20 million users worldwide.

IP: Internet protocol, a network layer protocol, was defined and is being further developed by the Internet Society Engineering Task Force (IETF), who rule the world.

ISDN: Integrated services digital network. A digital switched service originally developed by the telephone companies to allow higher speed services to be carried over the existing copper-based network. Euro-ISDN is a newer standard for ISDN: across Europe — either at basic rate or the faster 2Mbit/s primary rate. Now primarily associated with fibre-optic at the 'primary' rate. See **BRI** and **PRI**.

IT: Information technology refers to the computers, software and skills associated with processing information.

LAN: Local area network: The type of computer network typically used in a commercial environment, within and between adjacent buildings. LANs are normally based on communications technologies that are relatively high speed compared to traditional telephone company provided wide area networks.

Local loop: The connection between a customer's building and the local telephone exchange.

Lotus notes: A family of application tools enabling groups to share information in an easy to use way. Information is replicated on distributed servers.

Mosaic: A software program with a user friendly interface for accessing and navigating the Internet.

Multimedia: A generic term for any computer application which incorporates a meaningful combination of text, data, sound and vision. New multimedia applications are being developed for use over wide area networks.

Netscape: A software program with a user-friendly interface for accessing and navigating the Internet.

Open teleworking: This refers to teleworkers who place themselves and their services on the open market. In many senses they are subcontractors and as such have been around for a long time. However, with the advent of freely available computer technology and telecommunications it is likely that this type of teleworking will increase considerably and give rise to new markets, see **closed teleworking.**

PABX: Private automatic branch exchange is a telephone switch located on the customer's site which provides in-house telephony and access to the PSTN and/or private telephone network. Also known as PBX or sometimes just as a 'switch'.

PCMCIA: Personal Computer Memory Card International Association — a standard for credit card size intelligent add-on cards for PCs (eg for modems). Sometimes confusingly shortened to PC-card or Smart-card.

PDA: Personal digital assistant — the 'palmtop' size, next stage of sizing downward from notebook PC.

PNO: Public network operator, previously referred to as PTT, runs public telecommunications networks — see **Telcos.**

PRI: The ISDN **primary rate interface** offers 23 B-channels and a D-channel (23B+D) or 30 B-channels and a D-channel (30B+D).

PSTN: Public switched telephone network — the phone network.

Routers: Connect different types of LANs and WANs, help resolve addresses, decide the route packets take through the network, enforce output queue priorities, enable the network to be broken down into manageable domains, provide security barriers and fragment/reassemble large packets where necessary.

Security mechanism: One of many layers of security (eg encryption).

TCP: Transmission control protocol is a transport layer protocol which provides guaranteed delivery of packets. See also **IP**.

Telcos: Telephone companies.

Telebanking: A service which enables customers to phone a call centre and check their account balance, pay bills etc.

Telecentre: A telecentre is a place where more than one teleworker regularly carries out his or her work. Telecentres are usually linked to companies or corporate bodies which are devolving their central office functions.

Telecommuting: Telecommuting is the type of teleworking in which actual physical travel is avoided or minimised by the individual employee working from home using a PC and telecommunications. Telecommuting can be applied to nearly every job where face-to-face contact is not necessary at all times, and can provide substantial savings in travel cost and time. It is associated particularly with direct employment rather than freelance telework or outsourcing.

Telecottage: A telecottage is a centre usually involving more than one teleworker, usually located in a rural area, often with a community base which usually offers the normal range of business services, telecoms, business advice and work space and training. Telecottages are often funded or sponsored by organisations and companies in the initial start-up phase.

Tele-insurance: Selling insurance over the phone, cutting out the need for agents.

Telesales: Using call centres to sell products or services over the phone.

Teleworker: A teleworker is anyone who is working partly or totally from a home base or teleworking centre using a computer and telecommunications to carry out work activities.

UNIX: Became the *de facto* standard operating system for mini computers. Several variants exist.

Video-conferencing: Using telecommunications both to see and to talk to people at a remote location.

Virtual reality: The use of multimedia to create a simulation of a product or service so that a user can experience and interact with it (eg driving a car, climbing a mountain etc).

VPN: Virtual private network combines the features of a private network with the economy of scale and flexibility of using public switched services.

VSAT: Very small aperture terminals are small satellite dishes used to communicate via satellites. VSAT is suited to applications where the same information is broadcast to many sites, and also to reach remote locations.

WAN: Wide area network; a network which connects sites using a service provided by a PNO or Telco but otherwise is similar to a LAN.

Web browsing: The ability to find and look through the contents of a World Wide Web server on the Internet.

WWW: World Wide Web; a facility developed for the Internet, but also used on virtual private networks, which enables network servers to be set up containing hypertext files which when clicked on by a user will point them to other network files containing further, related information.

X.25: A type of packet switched network used extensively by PNOs for public services and popular for transaction based private networks, but now looking rather tired as compared to ATM.

Appendix D

Bibliography

Publications concerned with making flexible work happen, how to do it, and how others have done it.

Barrack, M (1992) *Flexiplace Questions and Answers on Computer and Telephone Issues*, General Services Administration, Washington DC, USA

Brain, D (1994) *Networking Small Businesses towards a New Economic Diversity*, ECTF, International Secretariat, FUE, Santa Cruz de Marcenado, 33-1-6, Madrid, Spain, Fax: +34 1 559 92 74

BT (1995) *Future Business*, British Telecommunications plc, Freefone 0800 800 887

CORNIX (1992) *Telnet — Guide to Teleworking*, CORNIX, 70 Causewayhead, Penzance, Cornwall TR18 2SR, Fax: +44 1736 69477

Coulson-Thomas, C and Coulson-Thomas, S (1990) *Implementing a Telecommuting Programme*, Rank Xerox UK Ltd (ISBN 0 9516900 0 0)

Coulson-Thomas, C (1994) *Business Process Re-engineering*, Kogan Page, London (ISBN 0 7494 1442 1)

Gray, M, Hodson, N and Gordon, G (1993) *Teleworking Explained*, John Wiley & Sons, Chichester (ISBN 0 471 93975 7)

Hafer, M (1992) *Telecommuting; An Alternative Route to Work — Training Guide II, WSEO-Washington State Energy Office*, Washington, DC

Harris, N (1992) *Flexible Working Practices — A Synopsis*, Digital Equipment Co Limited, The Crescent, Jays Close, Basingstoke, Hampshire RG22 4BS, Fax: +44 1489 882248

Krol, E (1994) *The Whole Internet,* O'Reilly & Associates, Inc, Sebastapol, CA 95472 (ISBN 1 56592 063 5)

Litinas, N (1993) *The Use of Telecommunications & IT for Stimulating the Development of SMEs in the Aegean Region*, ECTF, International Secretariat, FUE, Santa Cruz de Marcenado, 33-1-6, Madrid, Spain, Fax: +34 1 559 92 74

Markby, D (1993) *Guidelines for IT Management*, National Computing Centre (NCC) Ltd, Oxford Road, Manchester M1 7ED

Mitchell, H (1994) *DTI Teleworking Papers International Teleworking — Business Opportunities*, Brameur Ltd, London Tel: +44 1 252 313437

Nilles, J (1994) *Making Telecommuting Happen: A Guide for Telemanagers and Telecommuters*, VNR, California (ISBN 0-442-01857-6)

Page A, *et al* (1994) *Guidelines for Establishing a Regional Telework/Telematics Forum — 94: Version 1.4,* ECTF, International Secretariat, FUE, Santa Cruz de Marcenado, 33-1-6, Madrid, Spain, Fax: +34 1 559 92 74

Ridgewell, C (1993) *Making the Link between Workplace and Employee: Flexible Working Practices,* The European Distance Working Conference, The Home Office Partnership, Cambridge, Tel: +44 1 223 421911

Smart Valley Telecommuting Team (1994) *Smart Valley Telecommuting Guide*, 3Com Europe Limited, Wolsey Business Park, Tolpits Lane, Watford, Hertfordshire, WD1 8BL, Fax: +44 (0)1923 240446

3Com (1994) *Guide to Information Superhighways,* 3Com, Eaton Court, Maylands Avenue, Hemel Hempstead, Hertfordshire, HP2 7DF, Fax: +44 1442 275792

3Com (1994) *Guide to Teleworking,* 3Com, Eaton Court, Maylands Avenue, Hemel Hempstead, Hertfordshire, HP2 7DF, Fax: +44 1442 275792

3Com (1994) *Teleworking News,* 3Com, Eaton Court, Maylands Avenue, Hemel Hempstead, Hertfordshire, HP2 7DF, Fax: +44 1442 275792

Wendell, J (1992) *The Federal Flexible Workplace Pilot: Work at Home Component — Final Report,* Report No: PRD-92-15, US Office of Personnel Management, Washington, DC

Wiejers, T, Meijer, R, Spoel, E (1992) *Telework Remains Made to Measure: The Large Scale Introduction of Telework in The Netherlands* Butterworth-Heinemann Ltd, London

WSEO (1992) *Telecommuting: An Alternative Route to Work: Step-by-Step Guide Vol. I*, WSEO, Washington State Energy Office, Washington, DC

General discussions of flexible working and surveys of new working methods

Atkins, J *et al* (1994) *The Opportunity and Challenge of Telematics*, Labour Telematics Centre, Regional Technology Strategies Inc, RO Box 9005, Chapel Hill, North Carolina 27515–9005

Bakke, J W (1994) *Teleworking on the Domestic Scene*, Norwegian Telecom, Knausen 4, 2600, Norway

Barrera, E (1993) *Building a Europe for People. A Win-win Strategy?*,ECTF, International Secretariat, FUE, Santa Cruz de Marcenado, 33-1-6, Madrid, Spain, Fax: +34 1 559 92 74

Britton, FEK (1994) *New Concepts of Work in a Knowledge Society. The Telework Option Reviewed*, Office For Official Publications of the European Communities, L-2985, Luxembourg

Crichton, B (1993) *Corporate Transformation Flexible Working and the Opportunity for Rural Economic Developments*, Home Office Partnership, London, Tel: +44 1 223 421911

De Bony, E (1994–5) *Job Creation in the Information Society*, EC-DGXIII, Rue de la loi 200B-1049, Brussels, Belgium, E-mail: apas@postman.dg13.cec.be

EC (1990) *Review of Current Experiences and Prospects for Teleworking*, EC-DGXIII Rue de la loi 200 B-1049, Brussels, Belgium, E-mail: apas@postman.dg13.cec.be

EC (1994) *Growth Competition Employment: The Way Forward into the 21st Century*, Office For Official Publications of the European Communities, L-2985 Luxembourg (ISBN 92-826-7419-3)

ECTF/Govern Balear (1993) *The Resort Office of Europe: Seminar on Teleworking Tourism and the Balearic Islands as a Telematic Megapark*, ECTF/Govern Balear, International Secretariat, FUE, Santa Cruz de Marcenado, 33-1-6, Madrid, Spain, Fax: +34 1 559 92 74

Gonthier, D (1994–5) *The Digital World and Intellectual Property: Opportunities and Challenge — A Social Issue*, EC-DGXIII, Rue de la loi 200B-1049, Brussels, Belgium, E-mail: apas@postman.dg13.cec.be

Government Commission on IT (1994) *Information Technology: Wings to Human Ability,* Prime Minister's Office, Stockholm, Sweden (ISBN91- 38-13778-XISSNO375-250X)

Hunt, D (1994) *Telematic Trading: Towards the Global SME,* Babson, Boston, MA

Hurme, E (1995) *National Telework Development Programme,* The Danish National Telecommunications Authority, Helsinki, (ISBN 951-734-005-2)

Kinsman, F (1993) *The Future of Work,* Mercury Communications Ltd, New Mercury House, 26 Red Lion Square, London WC1R 4HQ, Fax: 0171 528 3517

Lecam, G (1993) *Moving Away From the Old Myth: How to Give Impetus to Both Human Resources as Well as Local Economic & Social Development,* The European Distance Working Conference, The Home Office Partnership, Cambridge, Tel: +44 223 421911

Molin, F (1992) *Teleworking Complexes and Networks as a New Regional Policy: The Case of the Balearic Islands,* ECTF, International Secretariat, FUE, Santa Cruz de Marcenado, 33-1-6, Madrid, Spain, Fax: +34 1 559 92 74

National Computer Board (1992) *A Vision of an Intelligent Island,* National Computer Board, Singapore (ISBN 981-00-3642-6)

Nilles, J (1992) *Concepts of Telework and Telecommuting,* JALA International, 971 Stonehill Lane, Los Angeles, CA 90049-1412, California, USA, Fax: +1 310 476 6007

Nilles, J (1992) *Telework and the Fate of Small Rural Communities,* JALA International, 971 Stonehill Lane, Los Angeles, CA 90049-1412, California, USA, Fax: +1 310 476 6007

Nilles, J (1993) *The Telecommunications – Transportation Tradeoff Options for Tomorrow and Today,* JALA International, 971 Stonehill Lane, Los Angeles, CA 90049–1412, California, USA, Fax: +1 310 476 6007

OFTEL Director General of Telecommunications (1993) *Interconnection and Accounting Separation Consultative Document,* OFTEL Director General of Telecommunications, 50 Ludgate Hill, London, EC4M 7JJ, Tel: +44 171634 8700

Overmars, J C (1994) *Report on the Round Table Conference on Growth Competitiveness and Employment*, Wierda Overmars & Partners, The Hague, The Netherlands, Fax: +31 70 350 566 1

Pekkola, J (1994) *Finnish Nordic and European Views to Telework and Need for Co-operation*, ECTF, International Secretariat, FUE, Santa Cruz de Marcenado, 33-1-6, Madrid, Spain, Fax: +34 1 559 92 74

Qvortrup, L (1992) 'Learning at a Distance', *CTSC International Newsletter*, Odense University, Denmark

Sociomics Ltd/Arkleton Trust (Research) Ltd (1994) *Employment Trends Related to the Use of Advanced Communications: Exploratory Investigation of Employment Trends in Rural Areas Related to ECS*, Office For Official Publications of the European Communities, L-2985, Luxembourg

Solon Consultants (1992) *Working at a Distance*, ISBN 0-9506340-1-8, Tel: +44 1 71 242 2261

Stern, E and Holti, R (1986) *Distance Working*, The Tavistock Institute of Human Relations, Office For Official Publications of the European Communities, L-2985 Luxembourg (ISBN 2 90 2940 04 1)

3Com (1995) *Europe and the Information Society*, 3Com, Eaton Court, Maylands Avenue, Hemel Hempstead, Hertfordshire HP2 7DF, Fax: +44 1442 275792

Wierda Overmars & Partners (1992) *Teleworking — Working by Telecommunication*, Scheveningen, The Netherlands, Fax: +31 70 350 5661

Research data from studies of flexible work, telework, telecommuting, business networking and allied topics

Bakke, J W (1993) *A Nordic Approach to Teleworking*, Telenor Research, Main Library, PO Box 83, N-2607 Kjeller, Norway

Bosworth, B and Rosenfeld, S (1992) *Significant Others; Exploring the Potential of Manufacturing Networks*, The Aspen Institute, Aspen, Colorado, USA

Bucciarelli, P (1994–5) *I&T Standards for the Information Society Greater Role, Greater Issues*, EC-DGXIII, Rue de la loi 200B-1049, Brussels, Belgium, E-mail: apas@postman.dg13.cec.be

De Bony, E (1994) *Global Networks and Interoperability: A priority in Europe's move to the Information Society*, EC-DGXIII, Rue de la loi 200B-1049, Brussels, Belgium, E-mail: apas@postman.dg13.cec.be

Dutton, W (1994) *The Information Superhighway: Britain's Response*, PICT Policy Research Papers No 29, PICT, London

Field, R (1994) *Evaluation of the ACOA/Enterprise Network*, Enterprise Networks, Newfoundland, Canada, E-mail: keith_sheppard @porthole. entnet.nf.ca

GMB College (1993) *Information Technology Electronic Communications and the Labour Market*, GMB College, College Road, Whalley Range, Manchester, M16 8BP, UK

Harris, R G (1991) *In Support of Communications, Competitiveness and Infrastructure Modernization Act of 1991*, United States Senate, Washington, DC, USA

Hollister, N (1995) *The Mobile Office — Towards the Virtual Corporation*, Financial Times Telecommunications & Media Publishing, London (ISBN 1 85334 273 4)

Huws, S and Robinson, U (1993) *An Exploratory Investigation of Contractual Arrangements for Telework Employment and Implications*, EC-DGXIII, Empirica, Oxfordstrasse 2, D53111, Bonn, Germany

Huws, U, Korte, W B and Robinson, S (1990) *Telework — Towards the Elusive Office*, John Wiley & Sons, Baffins Lane, Chichester, West Sussex PO19 1UD (ISBN 0 471 92284 6)

The Johns Hopkins University Institute for Policy Studies, *The Global Economy and Telecommunications: An Economic Development Seminar, Institute for Policy Studies*, The Johns Hopkins University, Baltimore, MD, USA

Julio, F and Chaparro, O (1991) *Autopistas Inteligentes Linares*, FUN-DESCO, Madrid (ISBN 84-8112-036-7)

Korte, W, Kordey, N and Robinson, S (1994–5) *Telework in Europe: Has It Lived up to Expectations?*, EC-DGXIII, Rue de la loi 200B-1049, Brussels, Belgium, E-mail: apas@postman.dg13.cec.be

Logica (1992) *Global Communications — Final Report: Opportunities for European and US Collaboration in Broadband Networking*, Logica, London

Longhorn, R (1994–5) *The Information Society Comparisons in the Trio of Europe, North America and Japan*, EC-DGXIII, Rue de la loi 200B-1049, Brussels, Belgium, E-mail: apas@postman.dg13.cec.be

Mattes, P (1994) *A Study of Folksam*, International Conference Teleworking, Strömstad, Sweden

Nilles, J (1988) *Traffic Reduction by Telecommuting: A Status Review and Selected Bibliography*, JALA International, 971 Stonehill Lane, Los Angeles, CA 90049-1412, California, USA, Fax: +1 310 476 6007

Nilles, J (1992) *Telecommuting Impact Forecasts*, JALA International, 971 Stonehill Lane, Los Angeles, CA 90049-1412, California, USA, Fax: +1 310 476 6007

Nilles, J (1992) *Telework: A History and Strategic Overview*, JALA International, 971 Stonehill Lane, Los Angeles, CA 90049-1412, California, USA, Fax: +1 310 476 6007

Nilles, J (1993) *City of Los Angeles Telecommuting Project — Final Report*, JALA International, 971 Stonehill Lane, Los Angeles, CA 90049-1412, California, USA, Fax: +1 310 476 6007

Nilles, J (1993) *Telecommuting and Traffic Reduction*, JALA International, 971 Stonehill Lane, Los Angeles, CA 90049-1412, California, USA, Fax: +1 310 476 6007

O'Neill, G (1993) *The Soft Revolution*, Henley Centre, Dublin, Ireland, Tel: +353 1 661 9147

Overmars, J, Jongerius, A and Hagenbeek, F (1994) *Report Telecommuting: Summary Conclusions and Recommendations*, RIV: A Department of the Ministry of Transport, Scheveningen, The Netherlands, Fax: +31 70 350 566 1

Paavonen, W (1993) *Swedish Teleworking Applications: Economical & Environmental Factors in Telework*, Paavonen Consulting AB, Helsinki

Page, A (1993) *Global Small Business — A Focus for Economic Recovery*, ECTF, International Secretariat, FUE, Santa Cruz de Marcenado, 33-1-6, Madrid, Spain, Fax: +34 1 559 92 74

PATRA (1993) *PATRA (Psychological Aspects of Teleworking in Rural Areas) A Review of the Literature*, PATRA, Department of Psychology, University of Wales, Swansea

Pekkola, J (1993) *Telework — A New Touch: Flexiwork Perspectives in the European and Nordic Labour Markets*, Ministry of Labour, Helsinki, Finland (ISBN951-47-8403-0ISSN0787-9393)

Pekkola, J (1993) *The History of Telework and the Use of the Labour Force at Two Finnish Firms in the IT Industry*, ECTF, International Secretariat, FUE, Santa Cruz de Marcenado, 33-1-6, Madrid, Spain, Fax: +34 1 559 92 74

Stanworth, J and Stanworth, C (1991) *Telework — The Human Resource Implications*, The Institute of Personnel Management, IPM House, Camp Road, Wimbledon, London SW19 4UX (ISBN 085292 465 8)

Stanworth, C, Stanworth, J and Purdy, D (1993) *Self-Employment and Labour-market Restructuring*, University of Westminster, London, (ISBN 1 85919 025 1)

Storgaard, K (1993) *Telework The Local Community and Ways of Life, Scandinavian Housing & Planning Research, no 10*

Teknibank (1993) *The Impact of the Accelerated Adoption of Broadband Communications of the European Community Economy*, Office For Official Publications of the European Communities, L-2985, Luxembourg

3Com (1994) *Information Superhighways: Awareness Levels amongst UK Business Leaders*, 3Com Europe Ltd, Eaton Court, Maylands Avenue, Hemel Hempstead, Hertfordshire HP2 7DF, UK, Fax: +44 1442 275792

Wolff, M (1995) *Case Study, New Organisational Structures for Engineering and Architectural Design: The Evaluation of Opportunities for Highlands & Islands Enterprise-Final Report*, Michael Wolff Associates, The Dower House, Lethen, Nairn IV12 5PR, Tel: 01667 452123

Yap, C S (1993) *The Intelligent Island Experience: The Role of SMEs in Economic Development*, ECTF, International Secretariat, FUE, Santa Cruz de Marcenado, 33-1-6, Madrid, Spain, Fax: +34 1 559 92 74

Regular publications

The European Journal of Teleworking, Addico Cornix Teleworking, 70 Causewayhead, Penzance, Cornwall TR18 2SR, Fax: +44 (0)1736 69477

Flexibility — Business Innovation and Human Resource Management, The Home Office Partnership, Cambridge, UK, Tel: +44 223 421911, E-mail: 100325.743@compuserve.com

The Gordon Report, Gil Gordon Associates, 10 Donner Court, Monmouth Junction, New Jersey, Fax: +1 908 329 2703

Index